All About Guitar Pentatonics

Develop your technique and play in any key!

This book is intended for guitarists who are venturing into the world of soloing and improvising and who want a common-sense approach with a lot of new patterns and exercises with easy-to-understand theory.

There is a substantial amount of information about how to use pentatonic scales and tips along the way, with many of the concepts repeated in various ways to enhance understanding. The focus is on connecting pentatonic scales, patterns, and exercises in any key using the entire fretboard.

Pentatonic scales are perhaps the most widely used scales for soloing in most styles of guitar. The pentatonic scale is a five-note scale using two notes per string. These patterns can be connected to give a guitarist access to the entire fretboard in all major and minor keys.

In this book:

- Over 630 different patterns and exercises!
- Patterns ranging from beginner to advanced.
- Build massive technique.
- Play in any key over the entire fretboard.
- Easy, usable theory.
- No need to read music.
- Detailed diagrams and tablature.
- Connect and combine all pentatonic scales.
- Techniques such as alternate picking, economy picking, hammer-ons and pull-offs, string skipping, and arpeggio-like patterns are included.

Thank you for your support!

For more materials and a perfect companion to this book:

All About Blues Guitar

www.allaboutguitarbooks.com

Contents

How to Practice

Each section was designed to help you learn something about each of the 5 pentatonic scales using patterns and exercises which develop technique for building speed, improvising and creating solos.

Most of the beginning scale exercises are written from the 5th fret. This is a comfortable spot when learning and practicing an exercise. After an example is learned and practiced, play the exercise from many different positions on the neck for optimal results.

Using a metronome at a comfortable speed is recommended. You can use a metronome to keep the beat and subdivide your playing into eight notes, sixteenths, or triplets. Or set the metronome at a higher speed using one click per note.

All of the examples are first presented with alternate picking and then again with hammer-ons and pull-offs. Strict alternate picking is usually the best for the picking exercises, but in some cases, economy or sweep picking works really well. Below are some examples to help understand when economy picking may be useful.

A combination like this would be common to sweep. But alternate picking is still very useful to practice on an example like this!

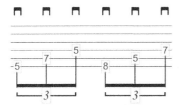

Descending sweeps. If practicing alternate picking, start with up.

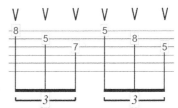

Economy picking really shines when hammer-ons and pull-offs are introduced. When alternating, continue to alternate after the hammer-on or pull-off.

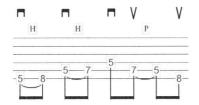

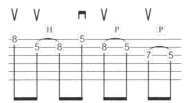

Sometimes, when skipping strings, alternate picking can be combined with economy picking. When skipping strings, alternate picking is usually the best choice. A natural arc occurs with alternate picking, which helps you avoid the string or strings you are attempting to skip.

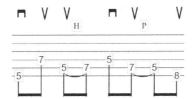

All Five Pentatonic Scales

These are the five pentatonic scale patterns used in the first sections of the book. As you progress through the book, you'll discover many new combinations of these patterns. The diagrams for the scale patterns below will be shown at the beginning of each section, so there is no need to memorize them now. Use this page mainly as a reference.

The patterns for major pentatonic and minor pentatonic are the same. They are numbered according to their relative position. Play the following patterns from many different frets. Use alternate picking.

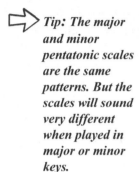

Tip: The major and minor pentatonic scales are the same patterns. But the scales will sound very different when played in major or minor keys.

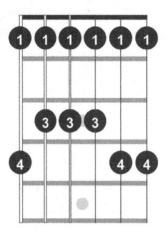

1 minor pentatonic
or
5 major pentatonic

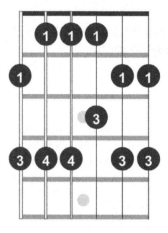

2 minor pentatonic
or
1 major pentatonic

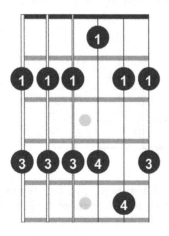

3 minor pentatonic
or
2 major pentatonic

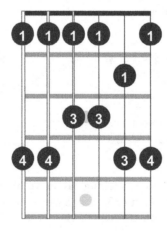

4 minor pentatonic
or
3 major pentatonic

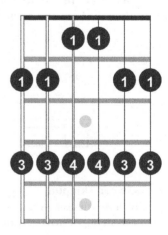

5 minor pentatonic
or
4 major pentatonic

Pentatonic Scale 1 or 5

Minor Pentatonic Scale 1 or Major Pentatonic 5

This is possibly the most widely used scale in guitar! This is because the pattern stays in position, making it easy to play and learn. This is pentatonic scale 1 in the sequence for minor keys or pentatonic 5 in the sequence for major keys.

To hear the scale as a minor scale, first pick a fret to play it from. The note on the 6th string that starts the scale is also the key you are in. For example, if you start from the 6th string, 5th fret, this would be A pentatonic in the key of A minor. Now play an Am chord, then the A pentatonic scale, and then the Am chord again. Or, record yourself playing an Am chord over and over and then play the A pentatonic scale along with the recording. You will hear that the scale fits the chord perfectly.

You can also play this scale over a group of chords in the same key. Search online or on a video sharing site for "backing track in A minor". You will find many examples of chords in key to play over. There are other ways to form searches, such as "Am backing track blues," "Am backing track country," "Am backing track jazz," "Am backing track metal," and so on. The music style doesn't matter. When playing over the chords from the backing track, just keep playing the scale even when you hear the backing chords change. The scale will still sound correct.

Try this trick! This minor pentatonic scale can also become major by playing it starting from the second note (pinky)! Starting from your first finger makes the scale minor, and starting from your pinky makes the scale major. This means there are two relative scales, one major and one minor, contained in the one scale pattern. Relative scales are scales that contain all the same notes, with each scale having a different starting point within that same group of notes. What makes them sound different is mostly the order of the backing chords. Usually, for the key of Am, the first chord is Am, and for the key of C major, C. Seek out backing tracks for the key of C major, line up your pinky on the note C (8th fret), and play. Now you are using the below scale pattern as a major pentatonic scale.

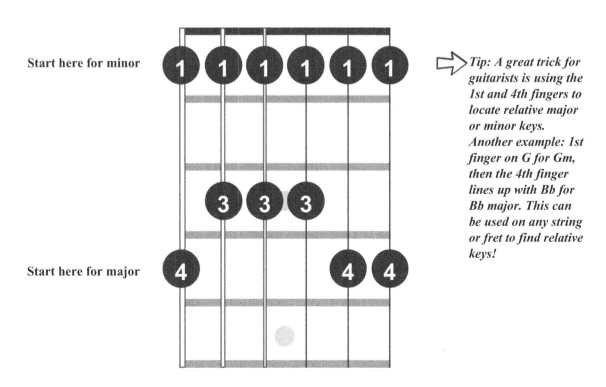

Tip: A great trick for guitarists is using the 1st and 4th fingers to locate relative major or minor keys. Another example: 1st finger on G for Gm, then the 4th finger lines up with Bb for Bb major. This can be used on any string or fret to find relative keys!

Unless otherwise specified, alternate pick, beginning with a down pick for ascending and an up pick for descending.

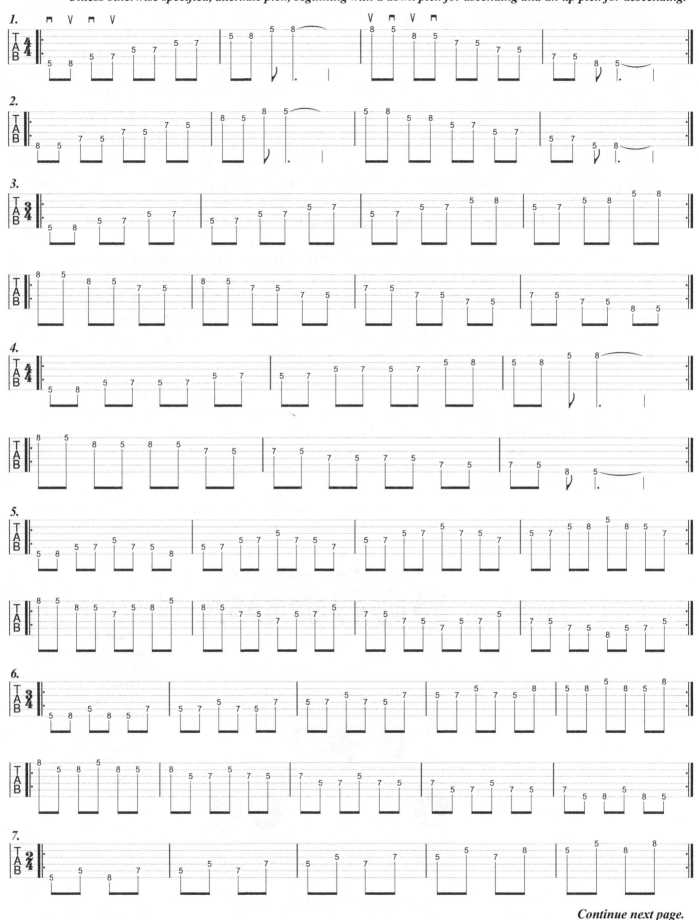

Continue next page.

➡️ *Tip: Jazz or Blues players may wish to swing the rhythms while practicing the scales and exercise patterns.*

If an exercise is too difficult, move on to another and come back to it later.

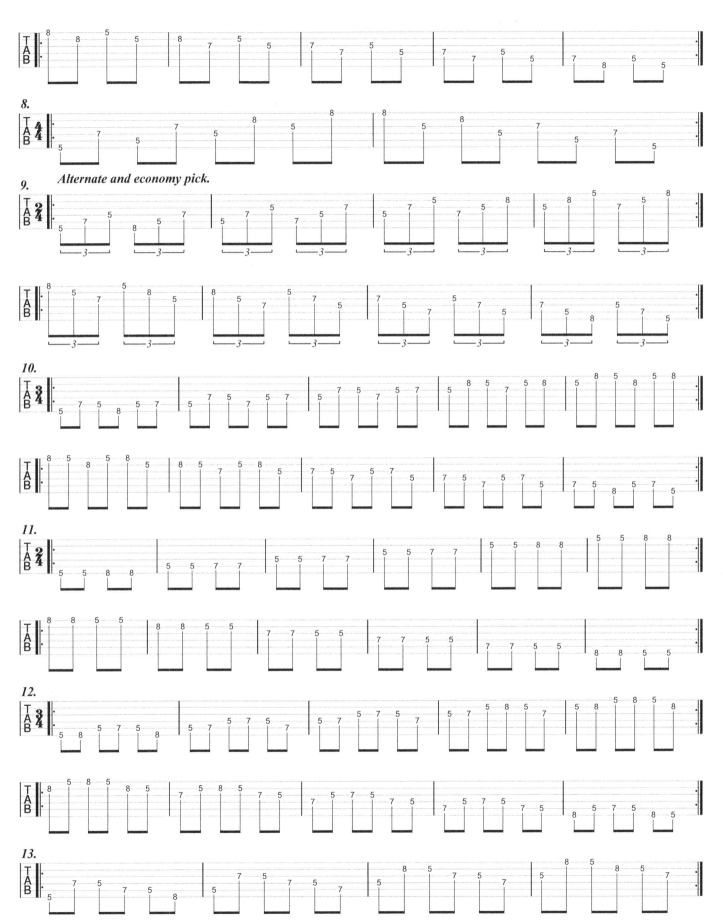

Sometimes, practicing one measure at a time can be a great exercise or riff on its own! Take your time.

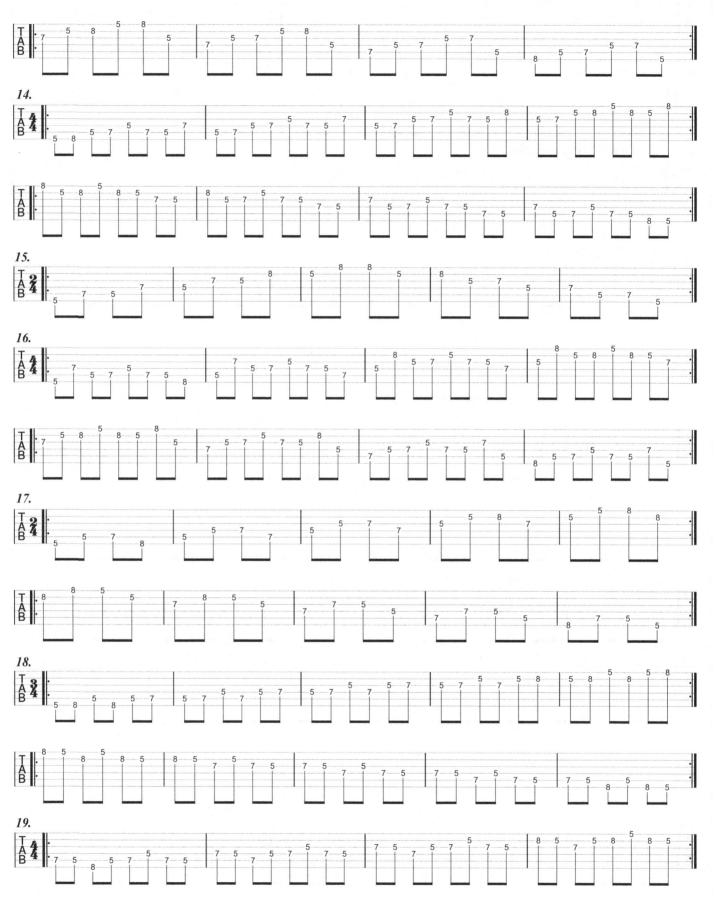

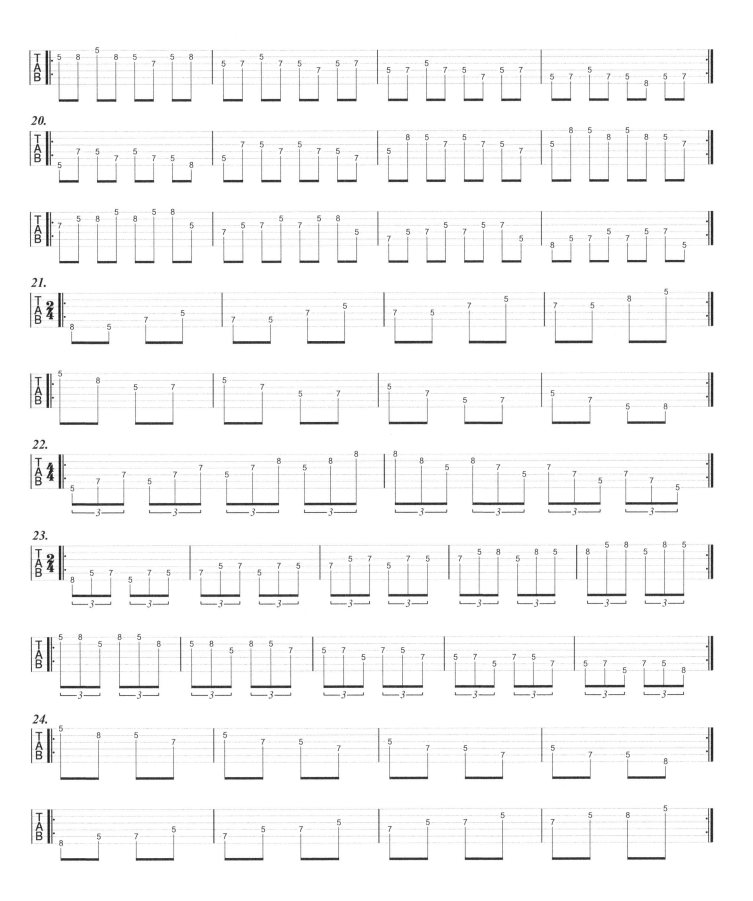

Hammer-on, pull-off version of the previous exercises. Picking may be alternate or economy between the hammer-ons and pull-offs. It is ideal to practice both ways!

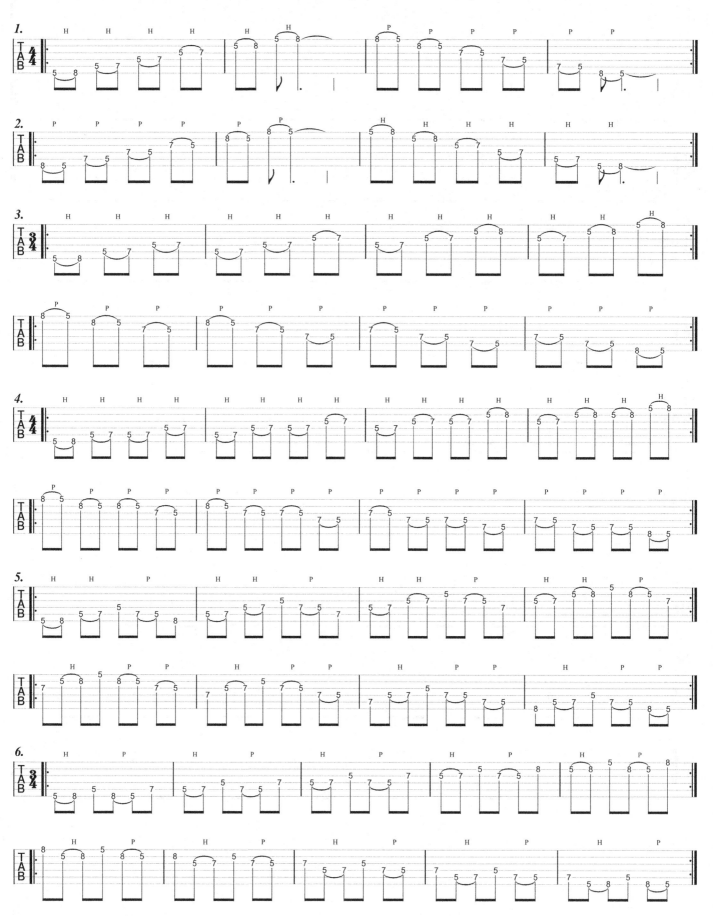

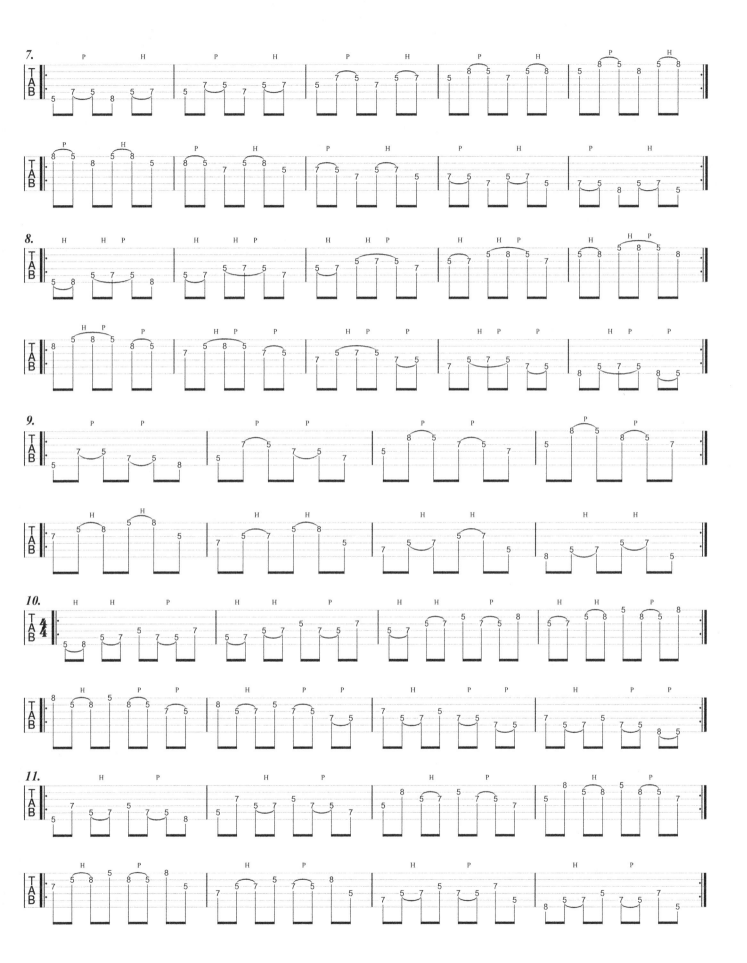

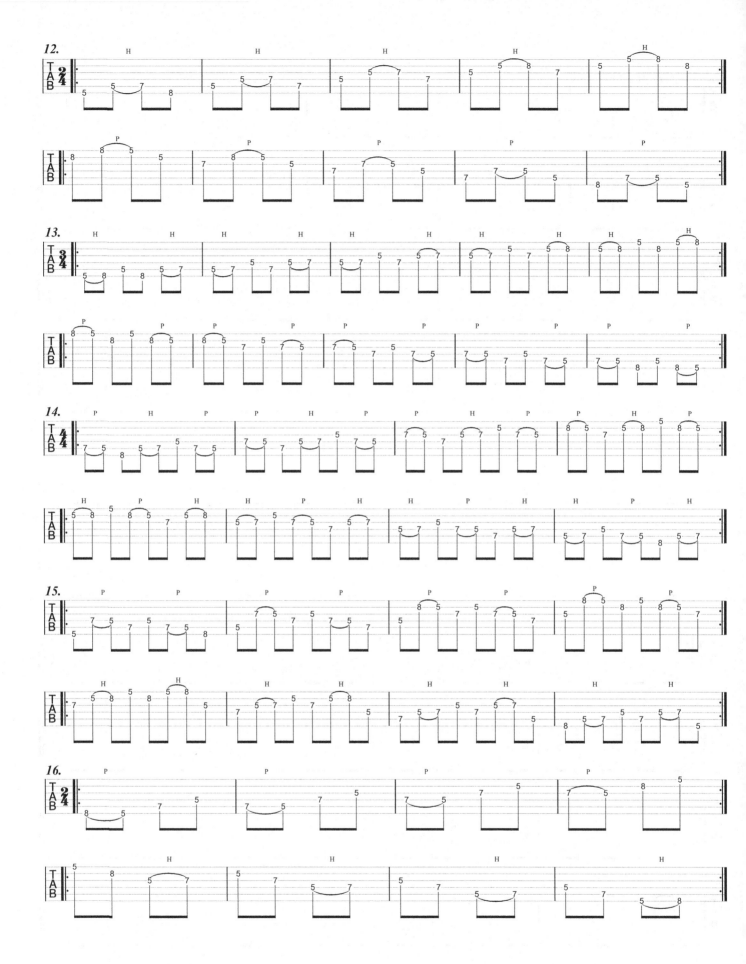

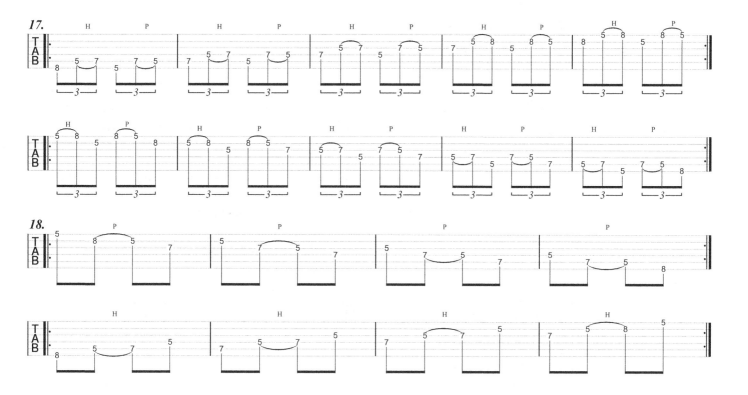

Pentatonic Scale 2 or 1
Minor Pentatonic Scale 2 or Major Pentatonic 1

This is the second scale in the pentatonic scale sequence for minor keys and the **first scale for major keys**. This scale is called **major pentatonic scale 1** because it is the first scale in the sequence for major keys and is often used to begin soloing in major keys. This scale also introduces **alternate fingerings**.

Major pentatonic scale 1 or Minor pentatonic scale 2

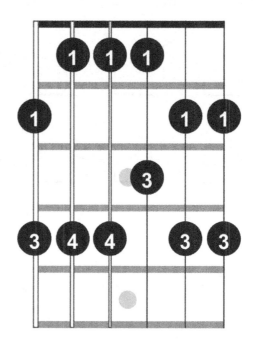

 Tip: Start at any fret on the 6th string and play minor pentatonic scale 1, but start with the 4th finger. Now play major pentatonic scale 1 from the same spot where the 4th finger was where you played minor pentatonic scale 1. Notice the notes are exactly the same for both scales. This is why starting on the 4th finger in minor pentatonic scale 1 is also major pentatonic scale 1.

Alternate Fingerings

The original scale fingering for the pentatonic scales is useful for many playing scenarios. However, in some situations when shifting up or down the fretboard or playing a tricky part of a solo, an alternate fingering may be necessary. Difficult musical passages can become much easier if you familiarize yourself with alternate fingerings. Not all possible alternate fingerings are listed. For example, all of the pentatonic scales can be played entirely with fingering 1-3, or replace all 1-3's with 1-2's and 1-4's with 1-3's.

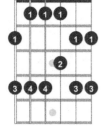 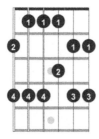 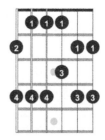 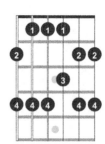

Many examples can be played with the original pentatonic scale fingerings. Sometimes you may have to stretch a little while using the original fingering. Use an alternate fingering if an exercise feels awkward. Alternate fingerings can also be combined with the original fingerings. Perfecting an exercise with more than one fingering provides the most flexibility when soloing.

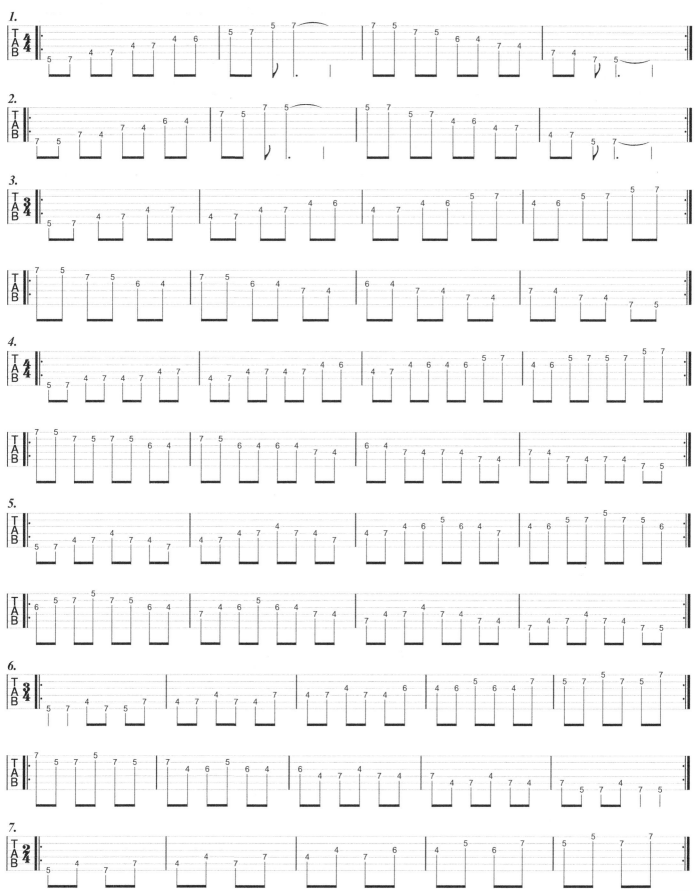

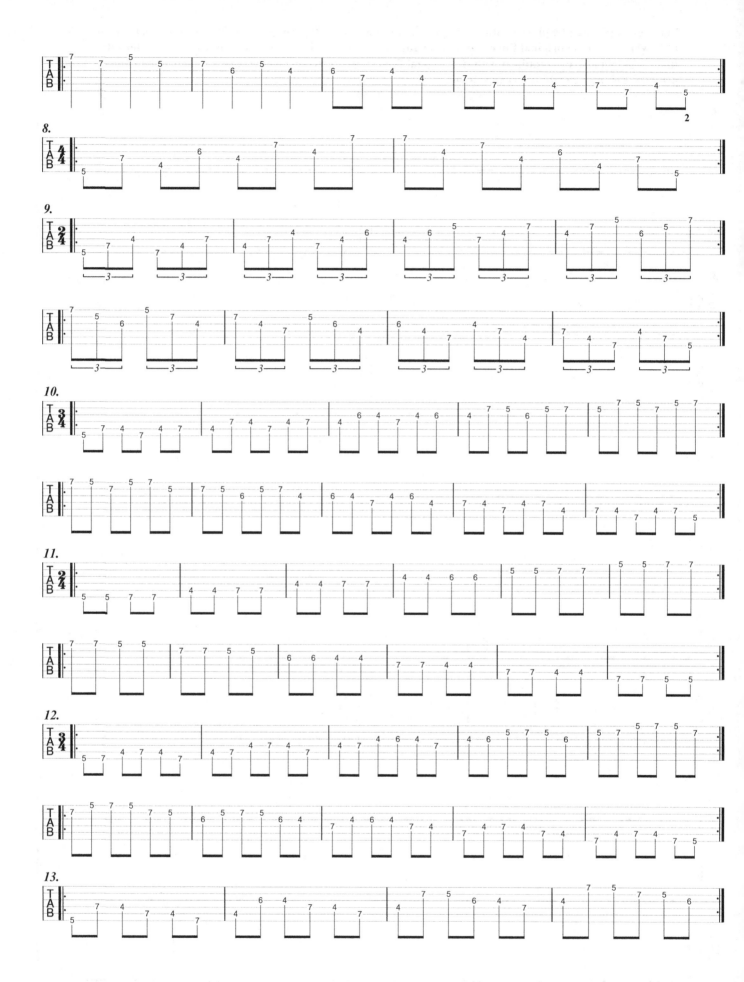

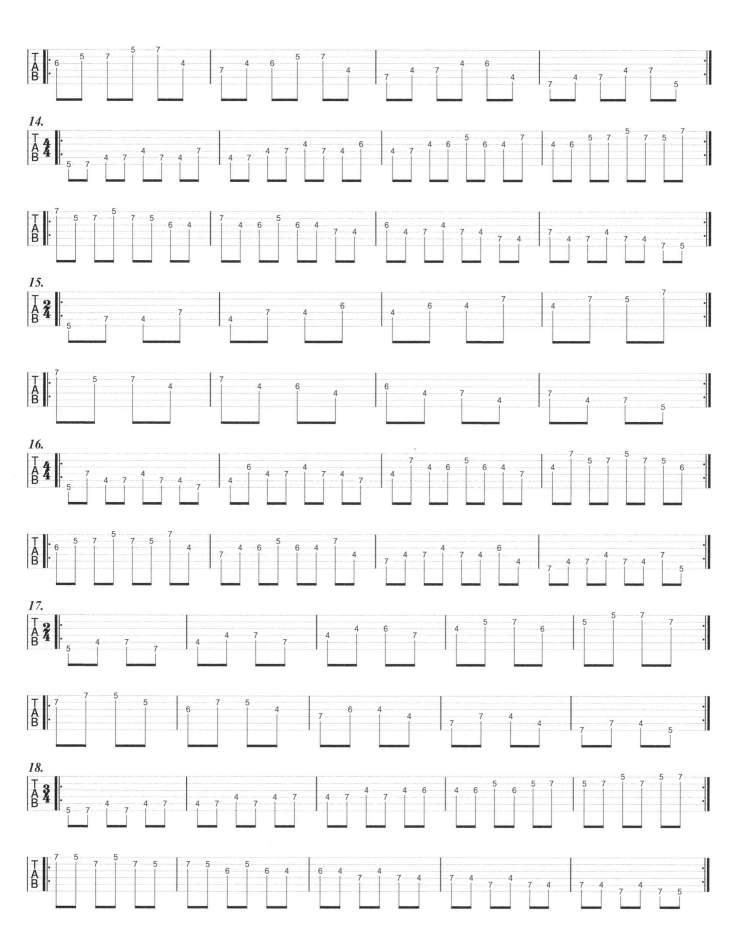

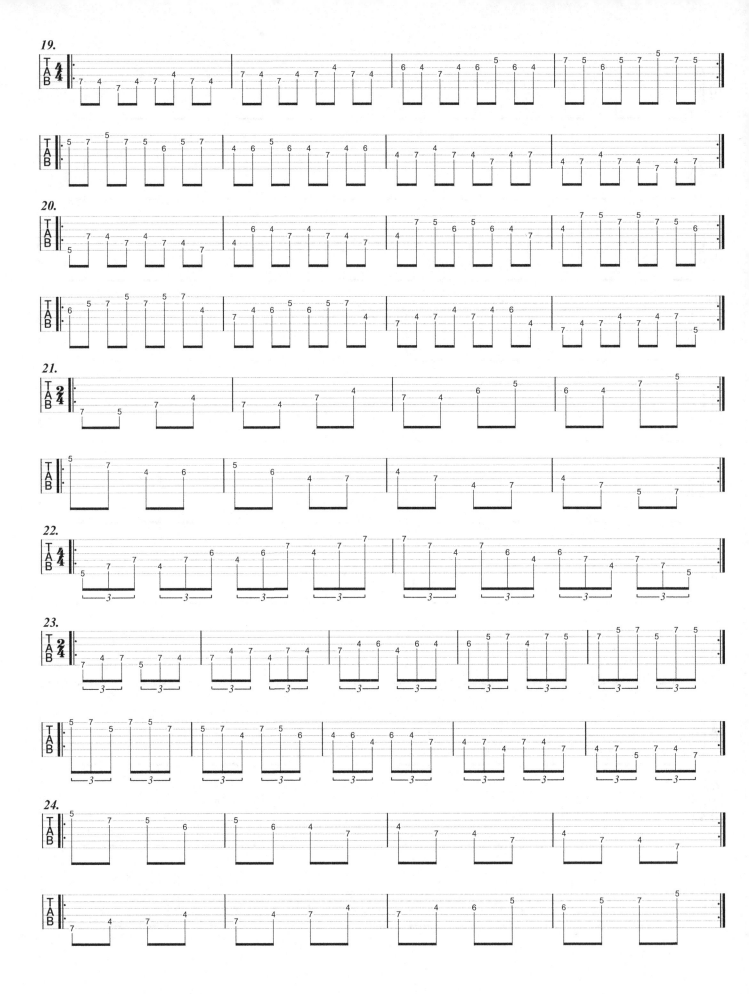

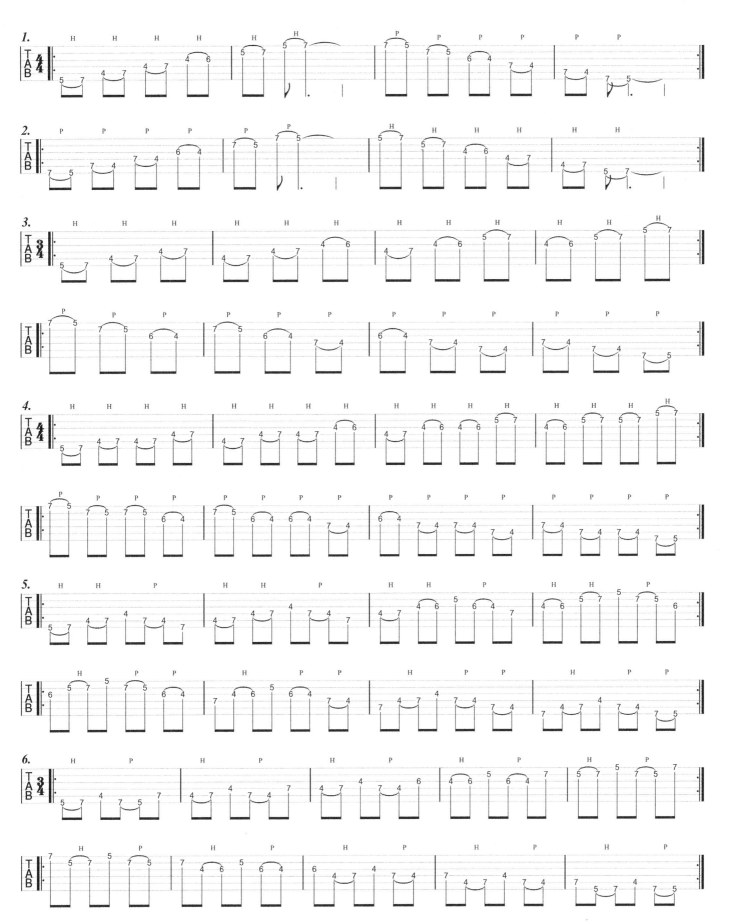

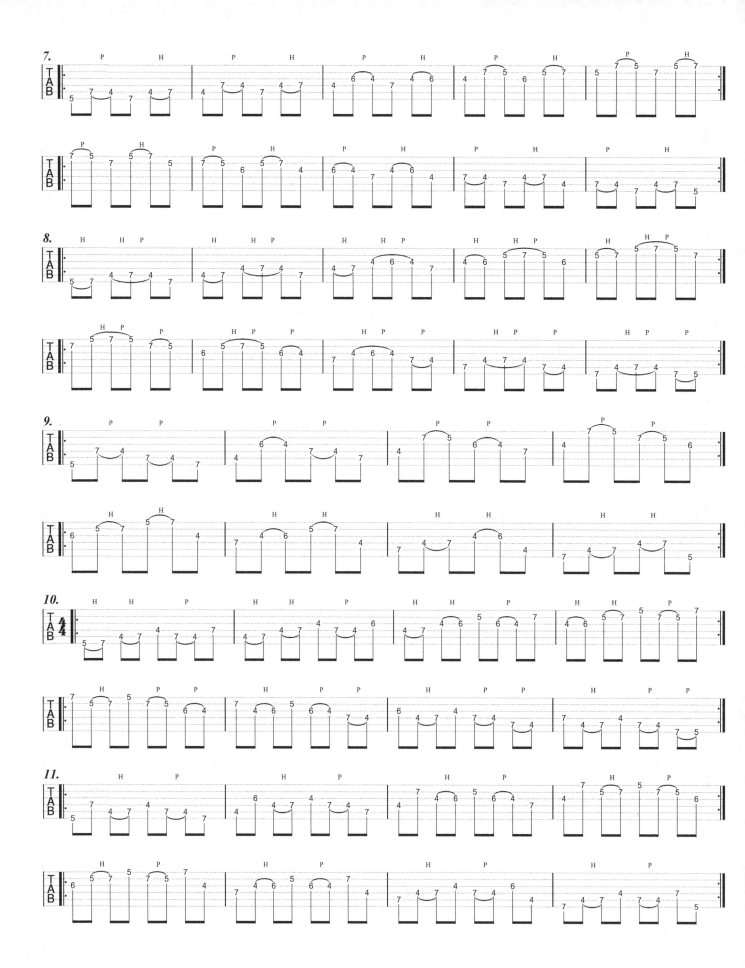

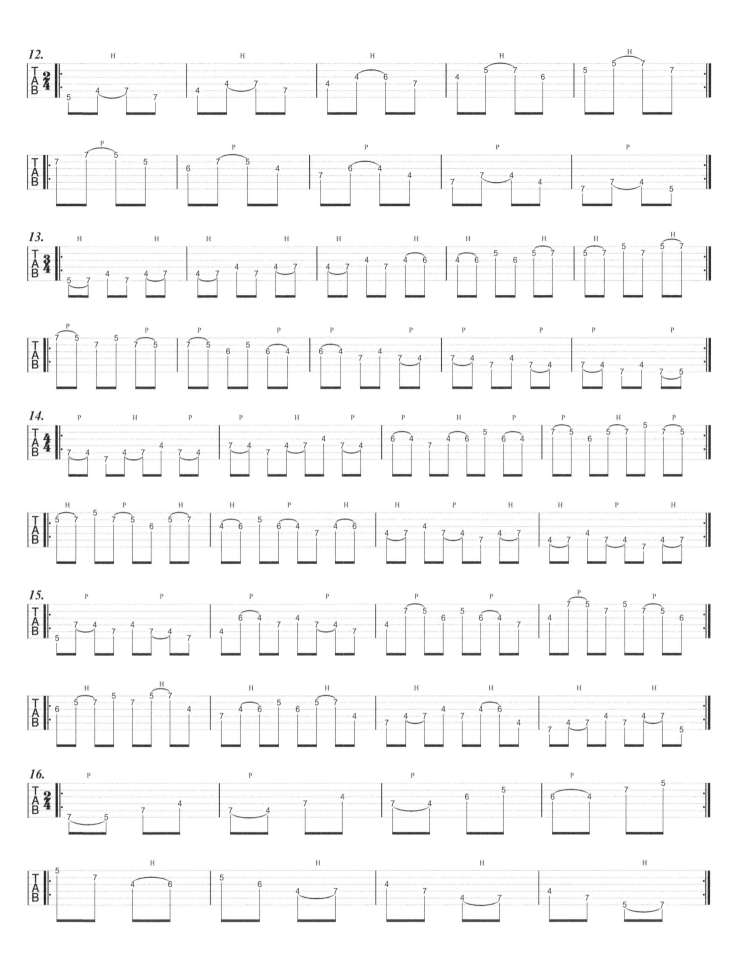

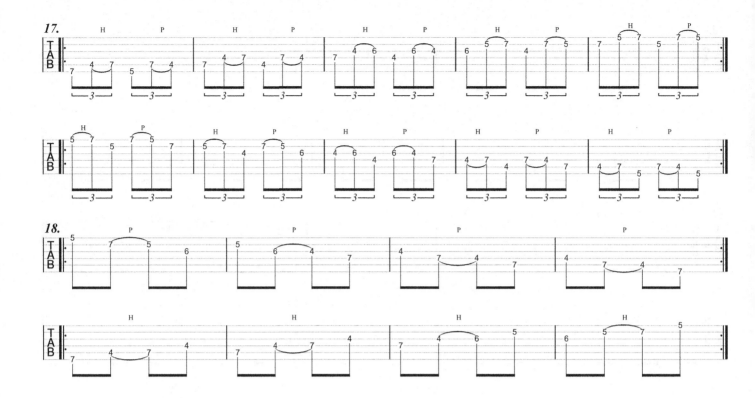

Pentatonic Scale 3 or 2

Minor Pentatonic Scale 3 or Major Pentatonic 2

This is the third scale in the pentatonic scale sequence for minor keys and the second scale for major keys. Look at the scale below and notice the beginning fingering of 1-3, 1-3 and 1-3 that occurs on the 6th, 5th and 4th strings. This is the same shape as in pentatonic scale 1, starting on the 5th string. This shape of 1-3, 1-3, and 1-3 also contains the same notes for both scales.

Same *shape* or fingerings

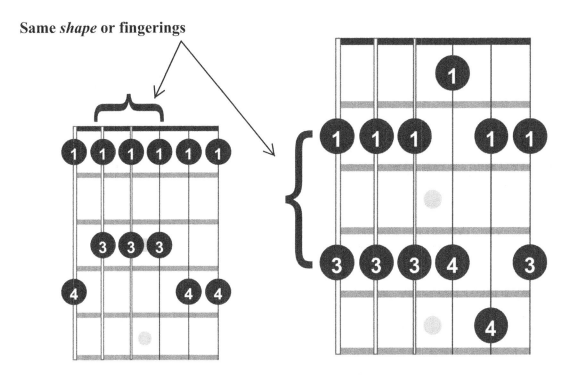

Alternate Fingerings

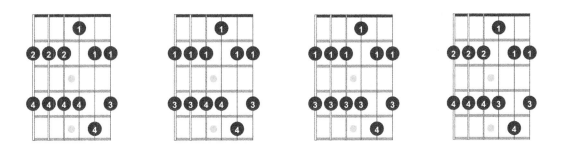

*Reminder: many examples can be played with the original fingering with a little stretch or with an alternate fingering. Perfecting an exercise with more than one fingering provides the most flexibility when soloing.

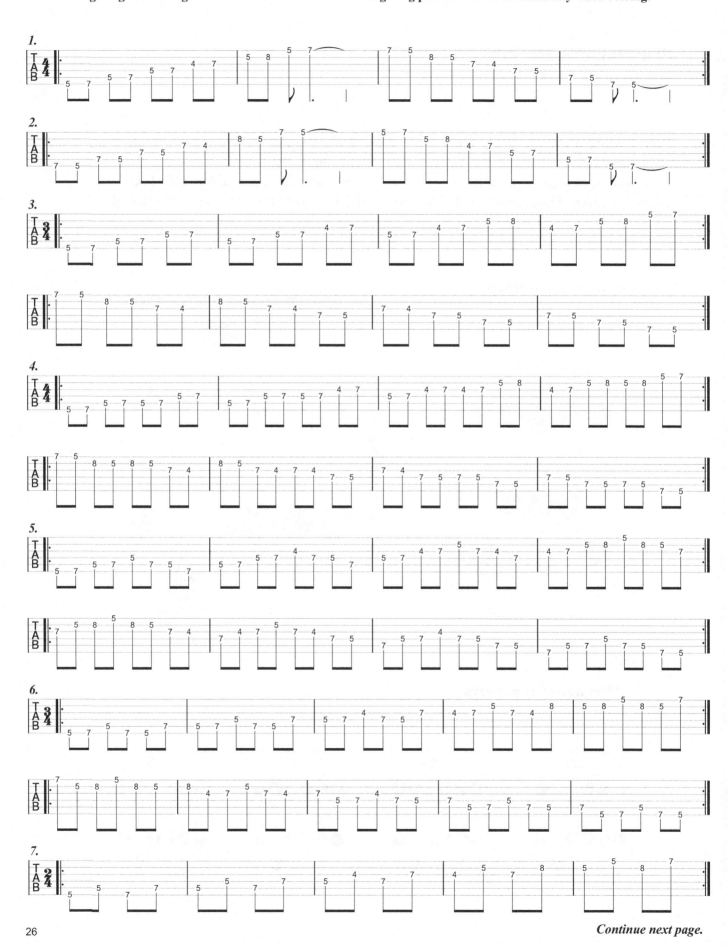

Continue next page.

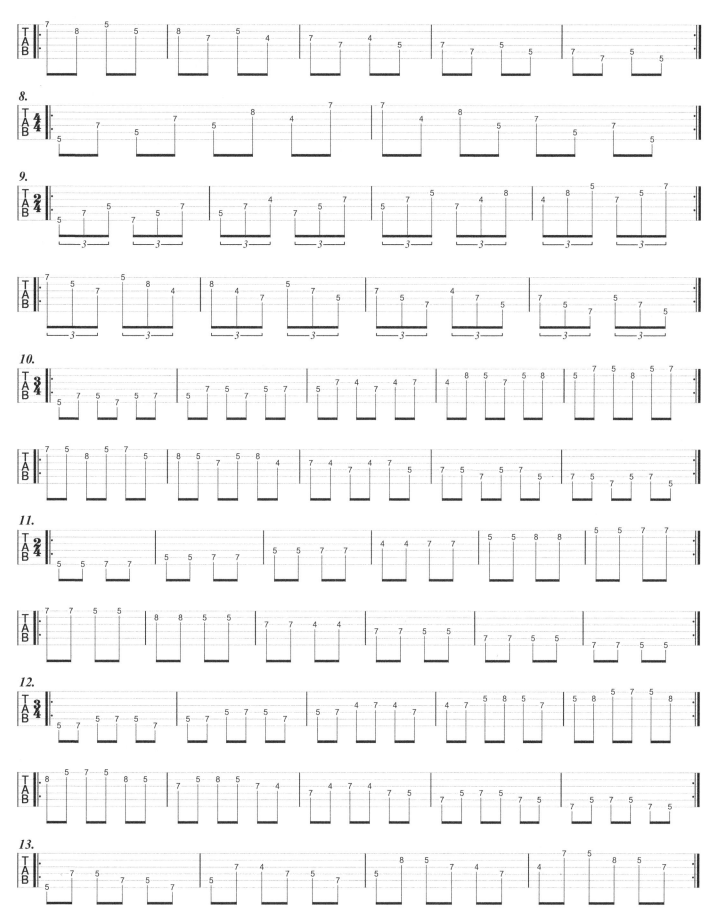

Continue next page.

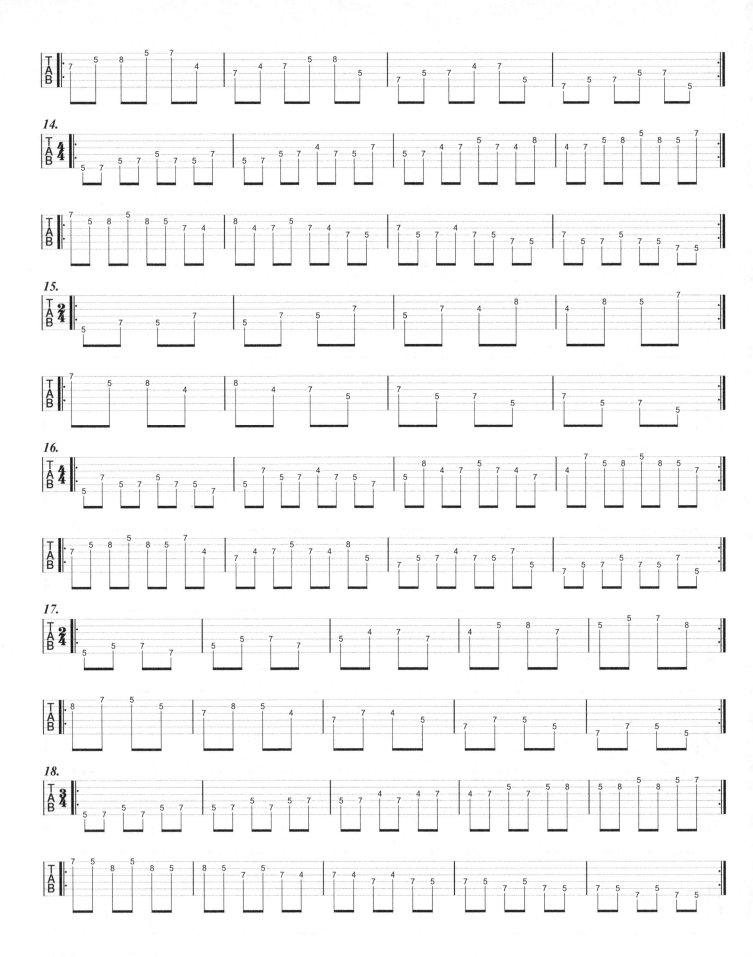

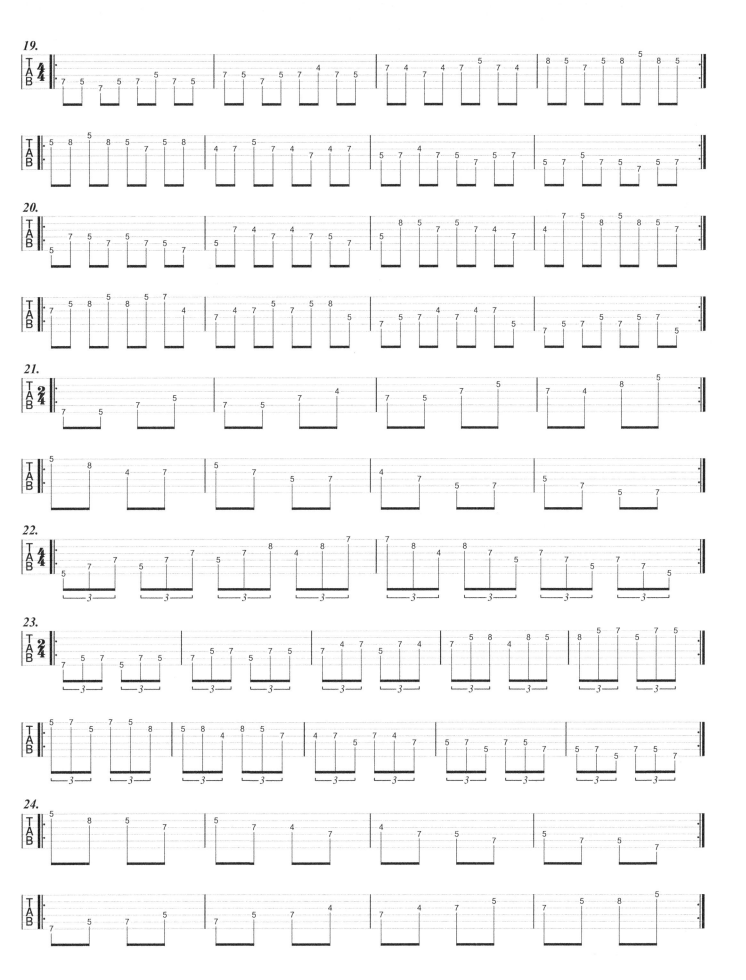

29

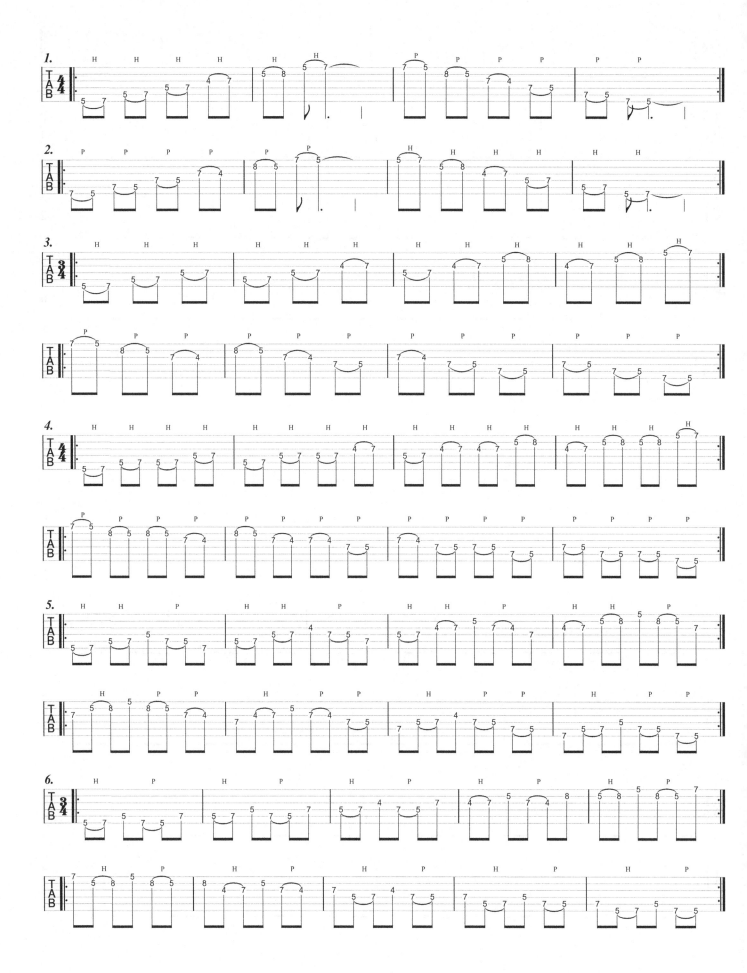

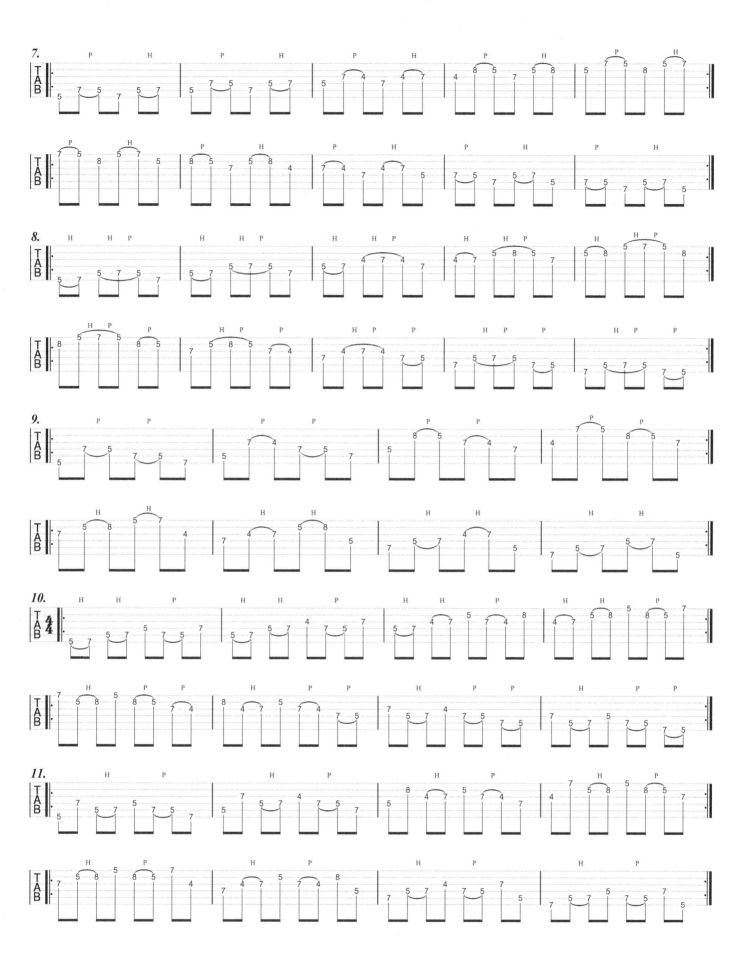

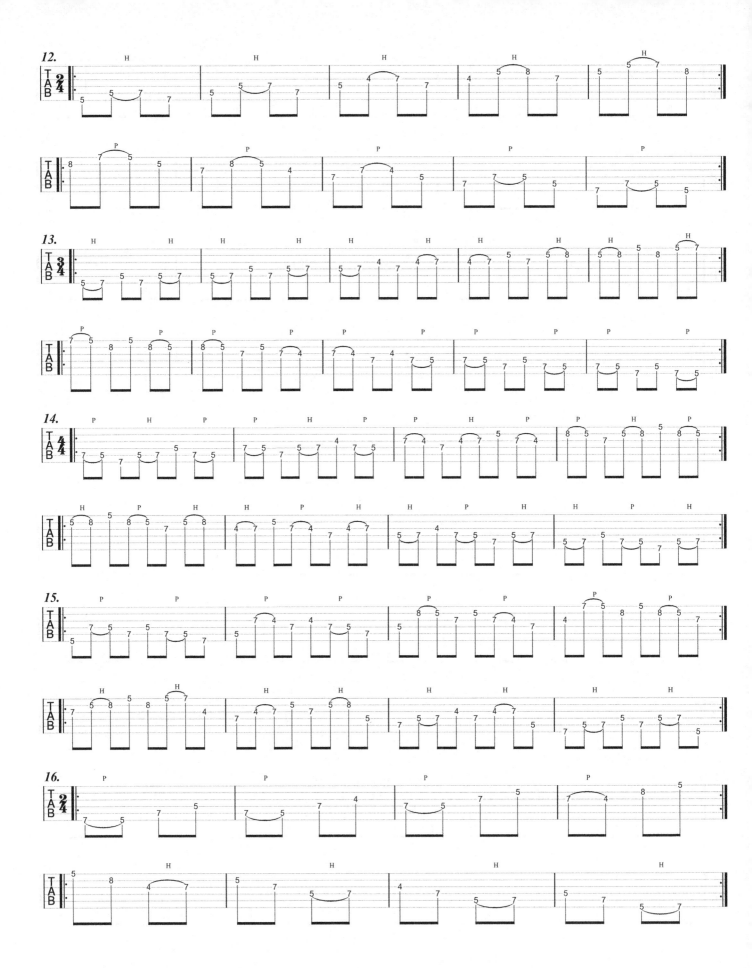

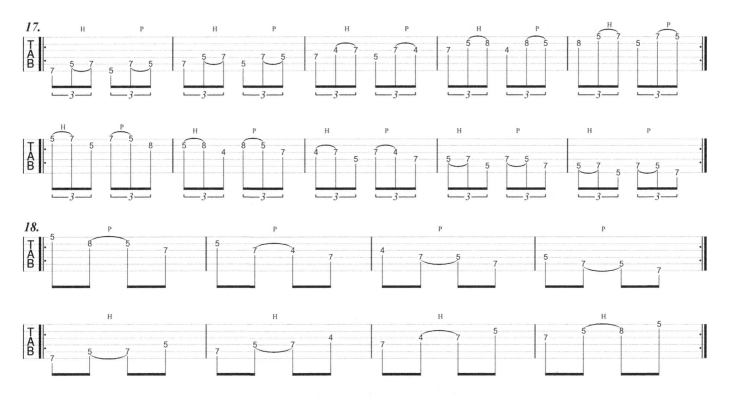

Pentatonic Scale 4 or 3

Minor Pentatonic Scale 4 or Major Pentatonic 3

This is the fourth scale in the pentatonic scale sequence for minor keys and the third scale for major keys. This scale pattern is very similar to pentatonic scale 1. In fact, you can see the fingering for minor pentatonic scale 1 starting on the 5th string below.

The 1-3, 1-3, 1-3 fingering is seen here again, but notice the last 1-3 is moved up a fret. This occurs because the interval distance between the open strings on the guitar is a fourth with the exception of the third to second string, G to B, which is a third. To make up for the third between the G and B strings, guitarists will have to move up a fret, making the distance a fourth when ascending to the second string and reversing by moving down a fret when descending.

1-3, 1-3, 1-3 fingering shape.

The last 1-3 is moved up a fret.

➡ *Tip: You can also think of this scale as a 5th string version of pentatonic scale 1 or 5.*

Alternate Fingerings

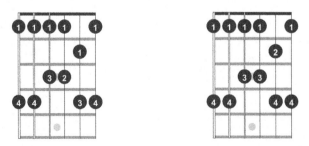

If an exercise is uncomfortable, try the alternate fingerings shown on the previous page.

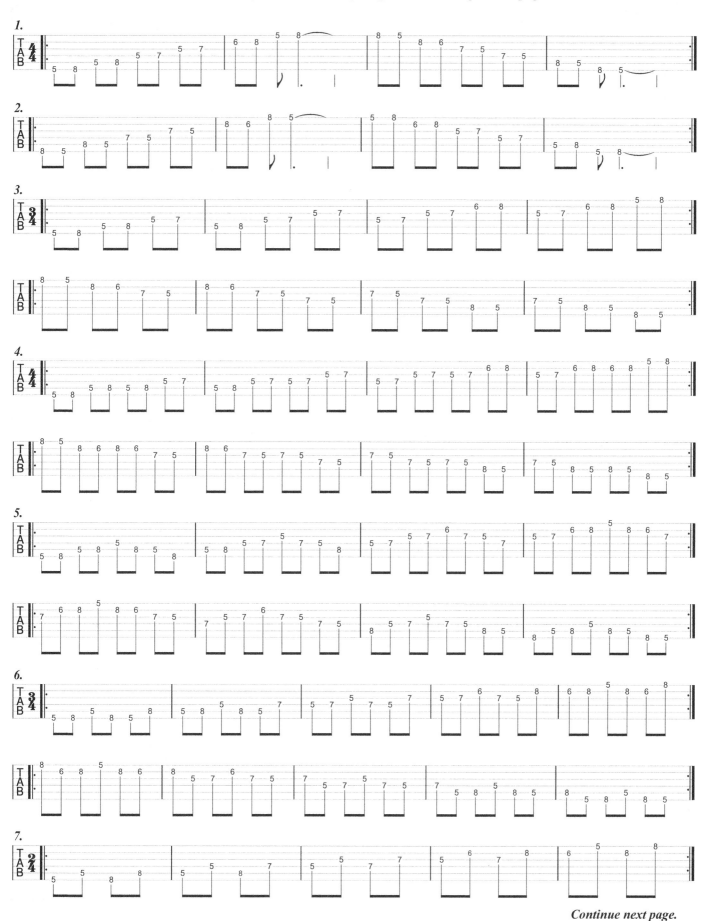

Continue next page.

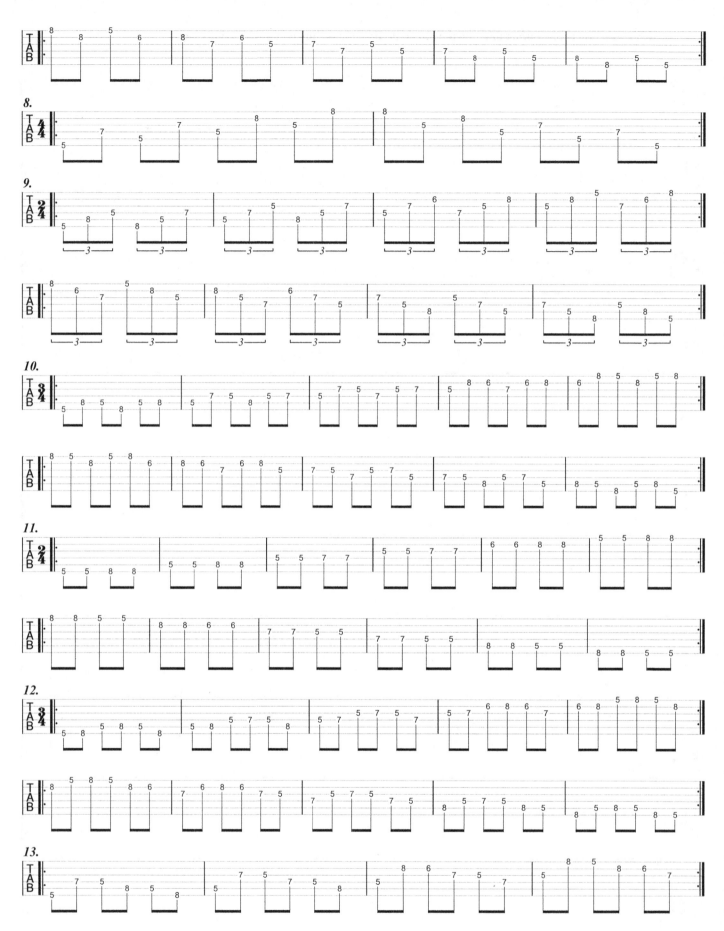

Continue next page.

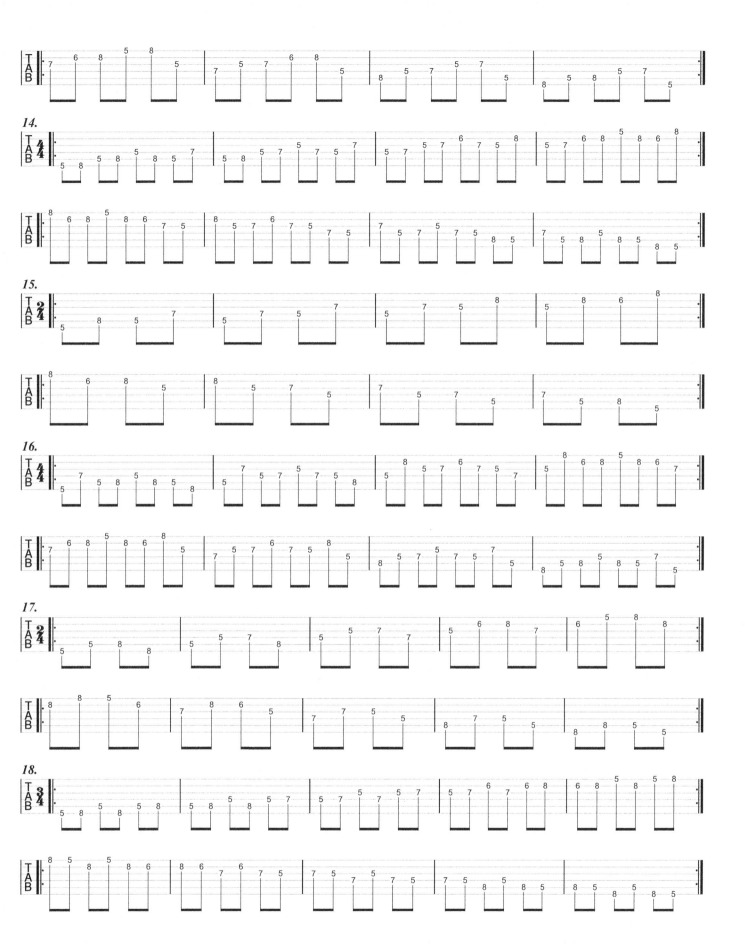

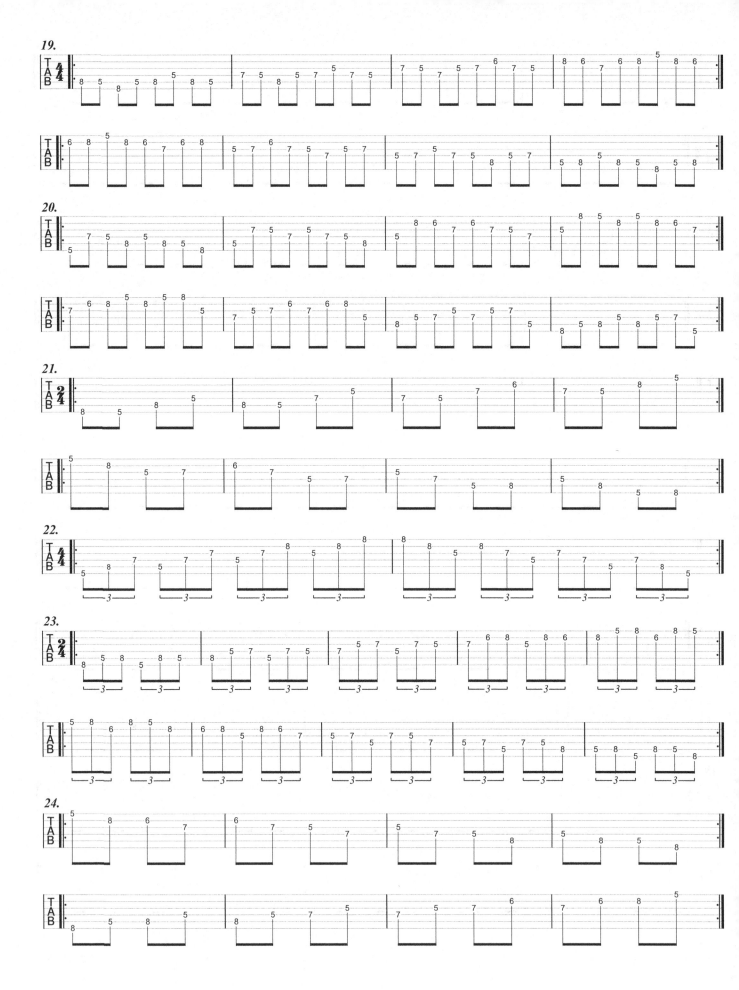

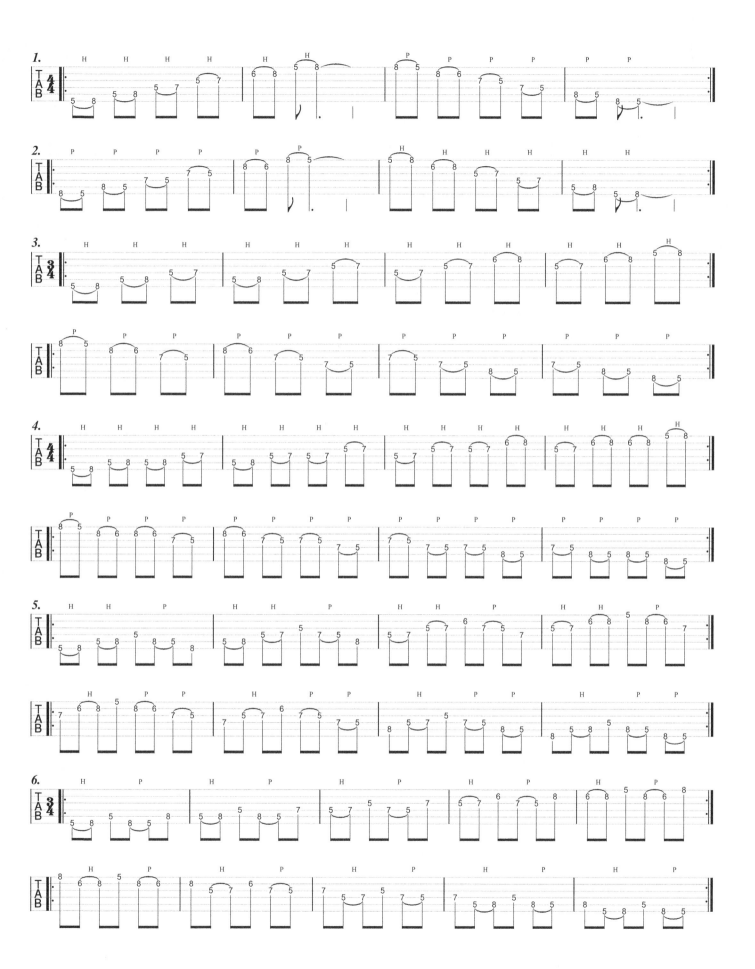

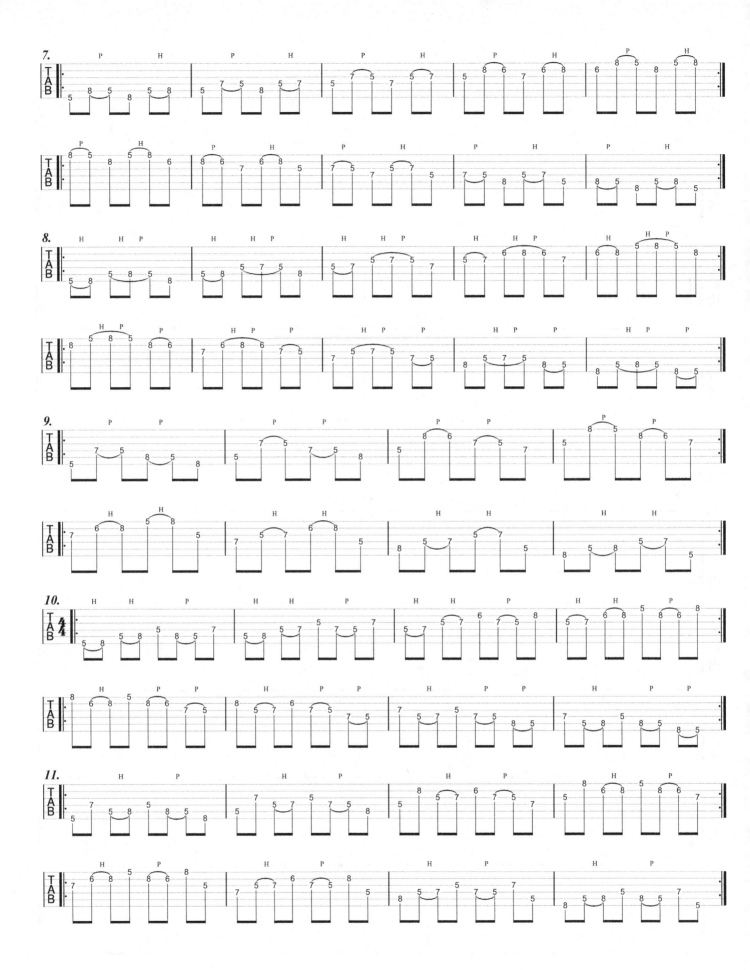

40

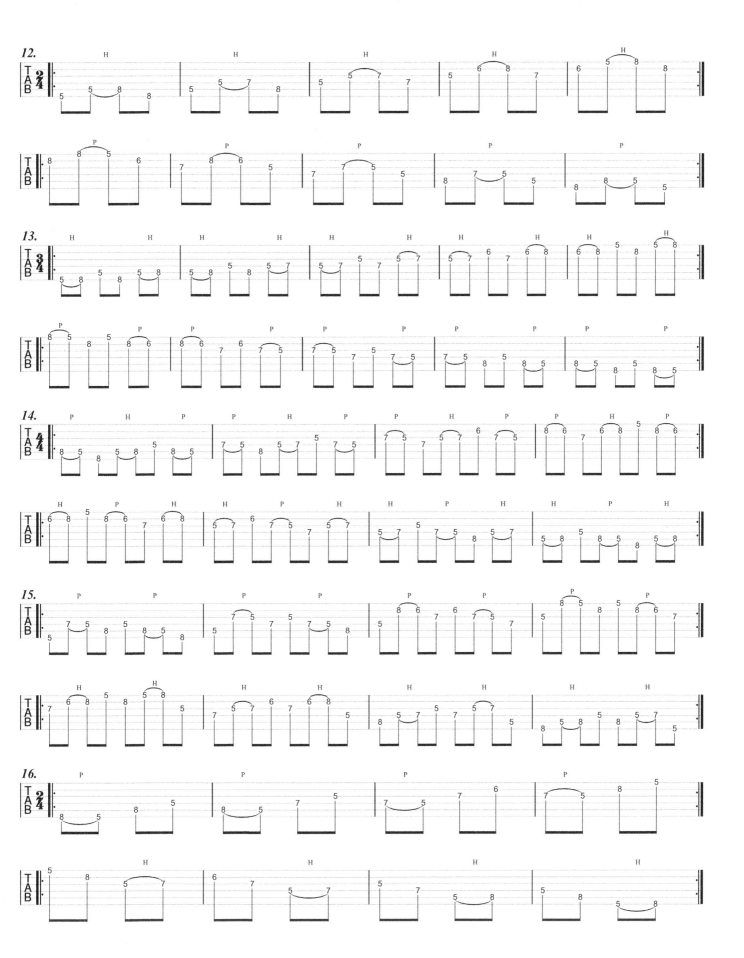

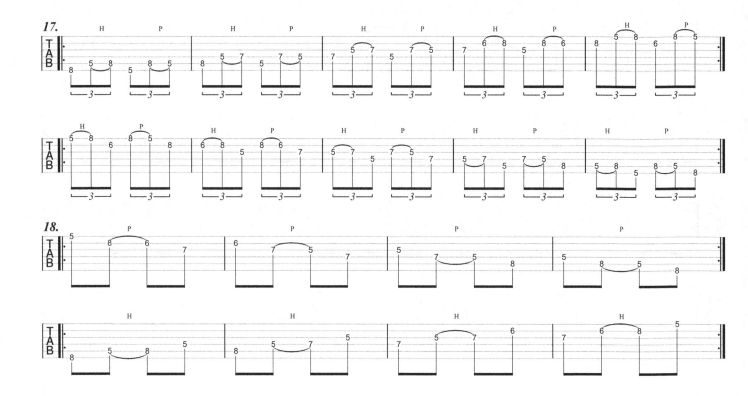

Pentatonic Scale 5 or 4

Minor Pentatonic Scale 5 or Major Pentatonic 4

This is the fifth scale in the pentatonic scale sequence for minor keys and the fourth scale for major keys. One of the easiest pentatonic scales to learn.

This 1-3, 1-3, 1-3 fingering pattern is not as noticeable here. That's because the pentatonic scales wrap around the fretboard. On the guitar, the 6th string and the 1st strings are both called E, and all of the notes have the same names on both strings. All of the pentatonic scales start and end with the same notes and frets on both the 6th and 1st string.

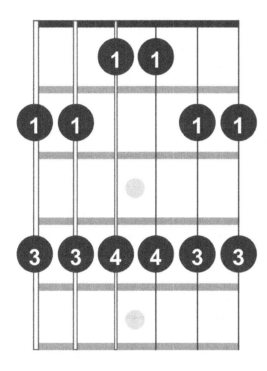

*1-3, 1-3, 1-3 fingering wraps around. The 1st and 6th strings are the same notes.

Alternate Fingerings

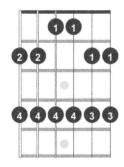
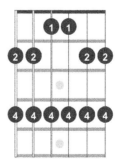

If an exercise is uncomfortable, try the alternate fingerings shown on the previous page.

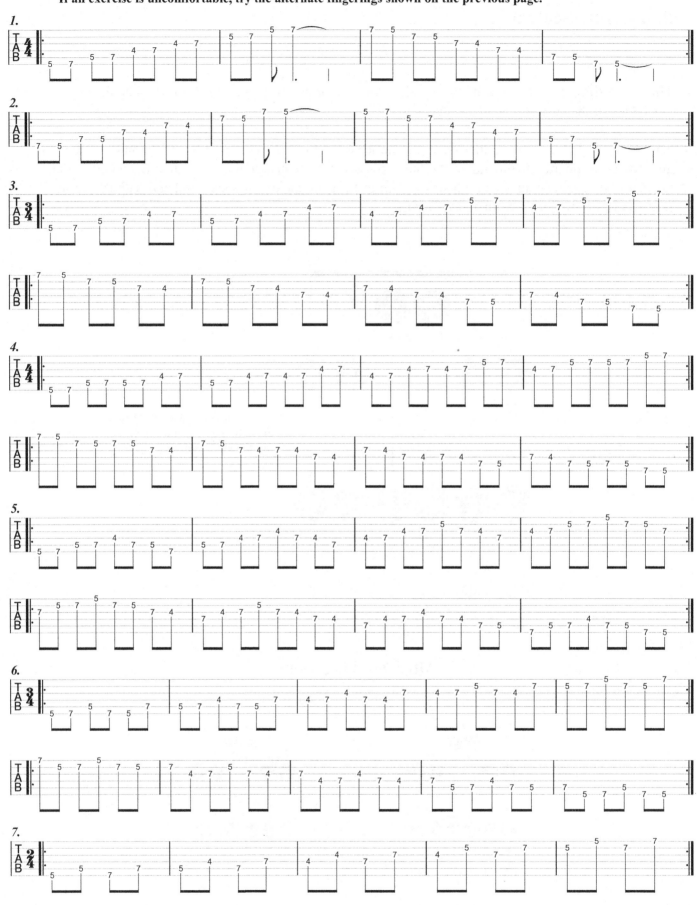

Continue next page.

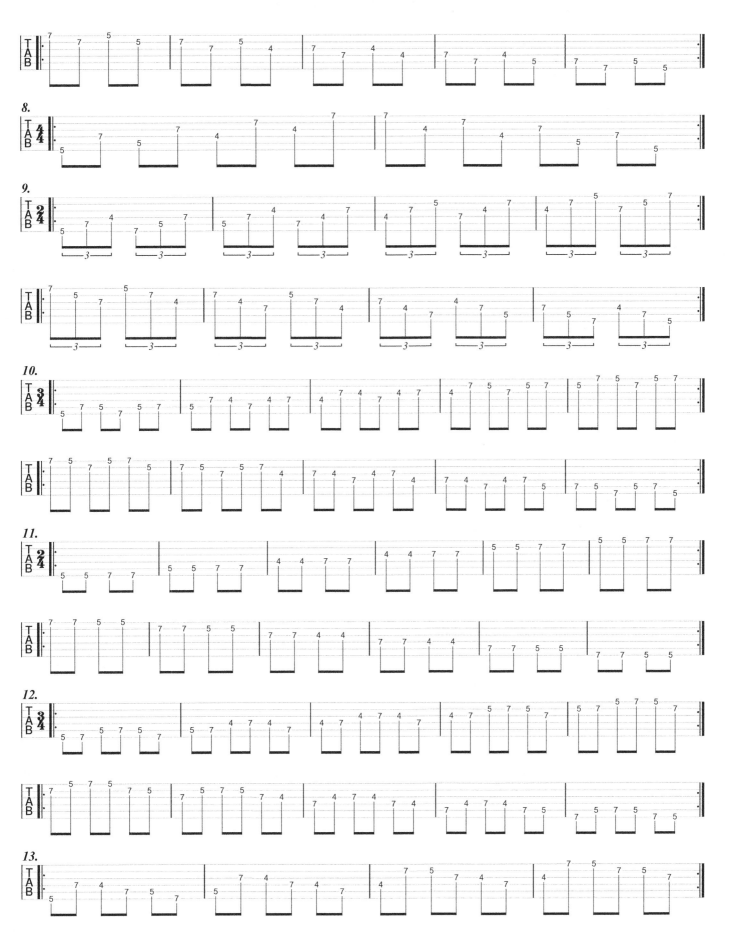

Continue next page.

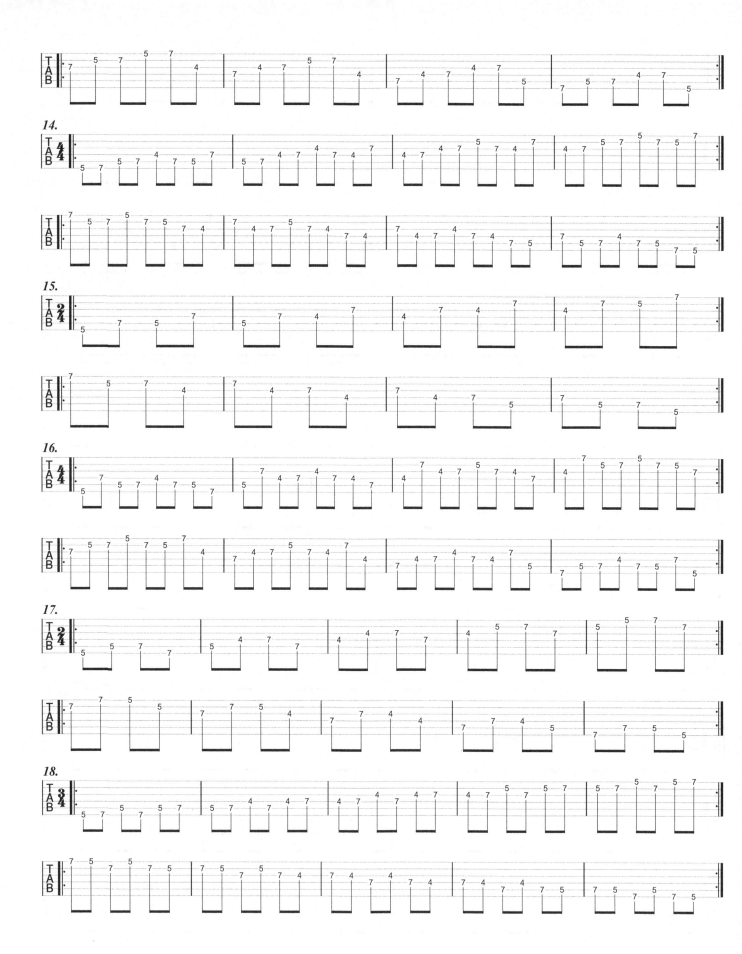

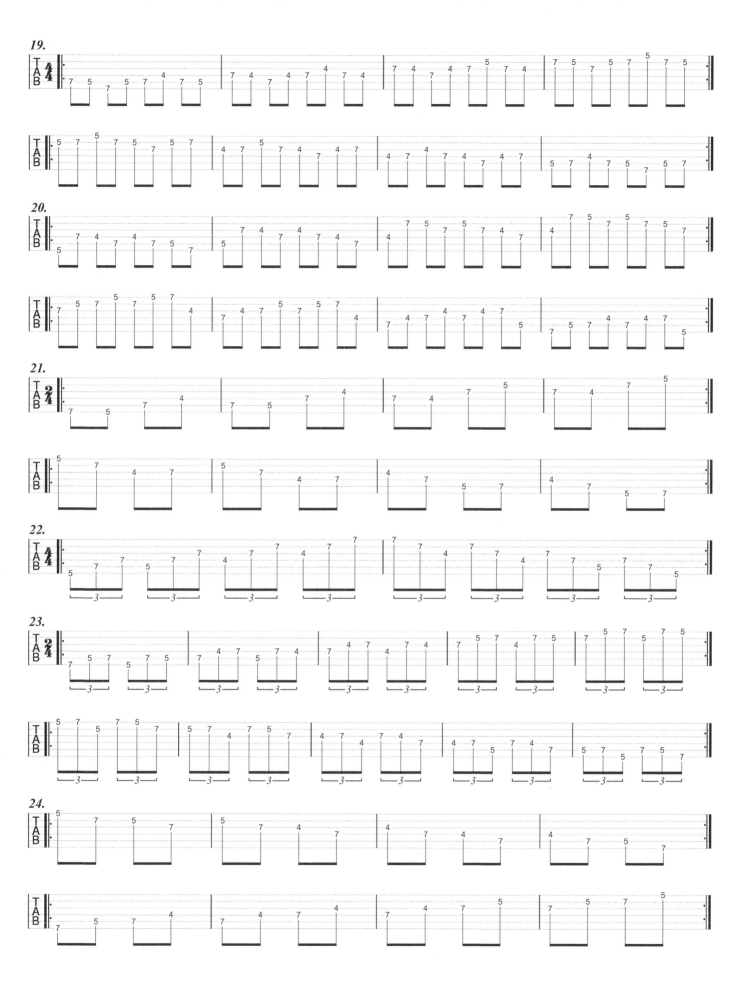

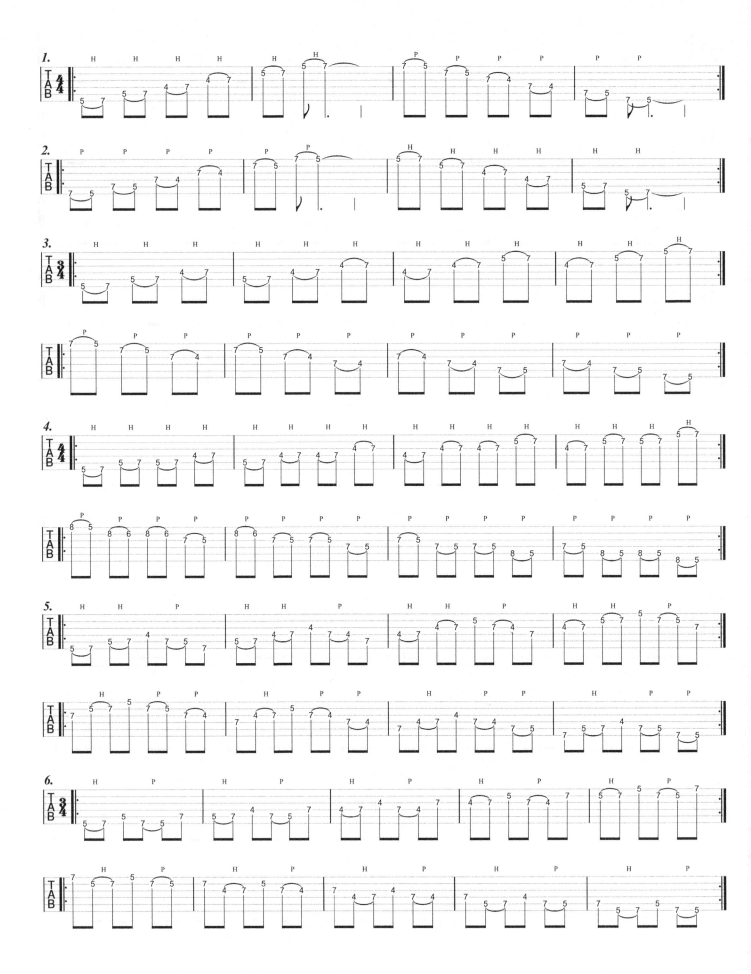

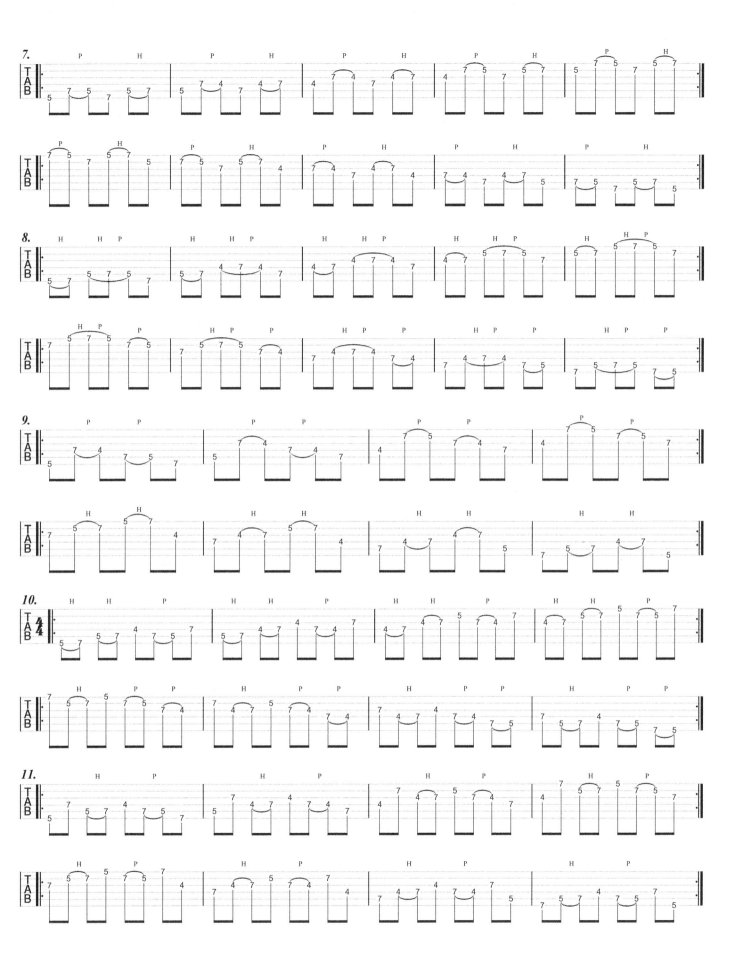

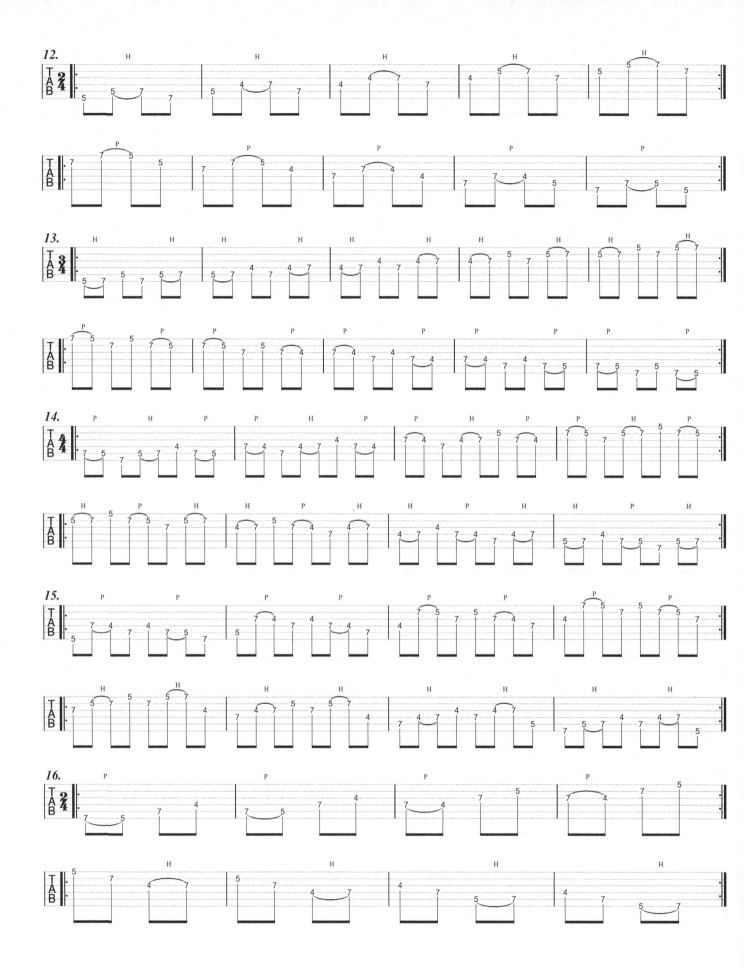

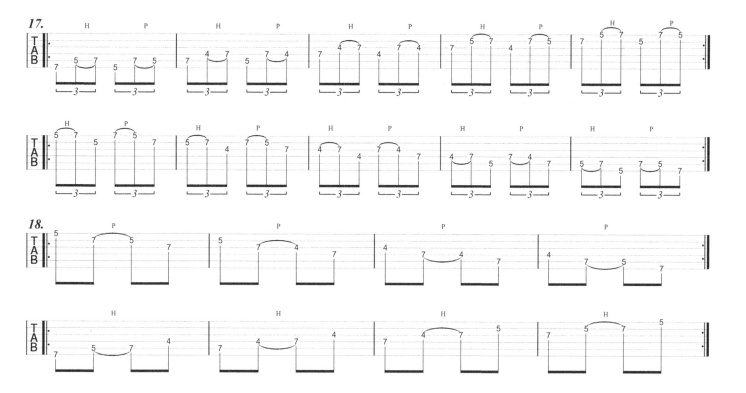

Connecting Pentatonic Scales I

There are many ways to combine and connect the pentatonic scales. This is necessary in order to play in key anywhere on the fretboard. You can begin with any pentatonic scale in any key, using any string or note within a pentatonic scale. Minor pentatonic scale 1 is a good place to start. For now, think of where you place your index finger on the 6th string as the starting note or root of the scale and the name of the key. The 'trick' mentioned earlier shows how to use minor pentatonic as major pentatonic using the same scale starting with your 4th finger. In the diagram below, the natural notes on the 6th string are shown (sharps and flats are between the natural notes). Use the diagram to find the major and minor pentatonic scales. Use minor pentatonic scale 1 with the 4th finger 'trick' to find major. **Of course, you can also use major pentatonic scale 1 to find major!**

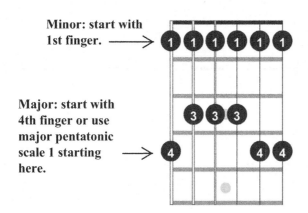

Minor: start with 1st finger. ⟶

Major: start with 4th finger or use major pentatonic scale 1 starting here. ⟶

Examples:

1. G minor pentatonic: 3rd fret, 1st finger

2. B minor pentatonic: 7th fret, 1st finger

3. C major pentatonic: 8th fret, 4th finger

4. A major pentatonic: 5th fret, 4th finger

5. F# minor pentatonic: 2nd fret, 1st finger

6. Bb major pentatonic: 6th fret, 4th finger

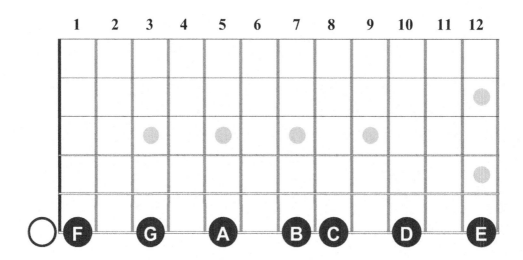

Find:

C minor pentatonic   D major pentatonic

E minor pentatonic   F major pentatonic

Connecting Pentatonic Scales II

The major pentatonic scales and minor pentatonic scales are the same patterns. The major or minor sound is greatly influenced by the chords or key you are playing in.

Below shows the pentatonic scales connected in sequence for major and minor.

The scales connect in the same way in relation to each other for both major and minor keys.

*Each scale is joined to the next by its second note on the 6th string.

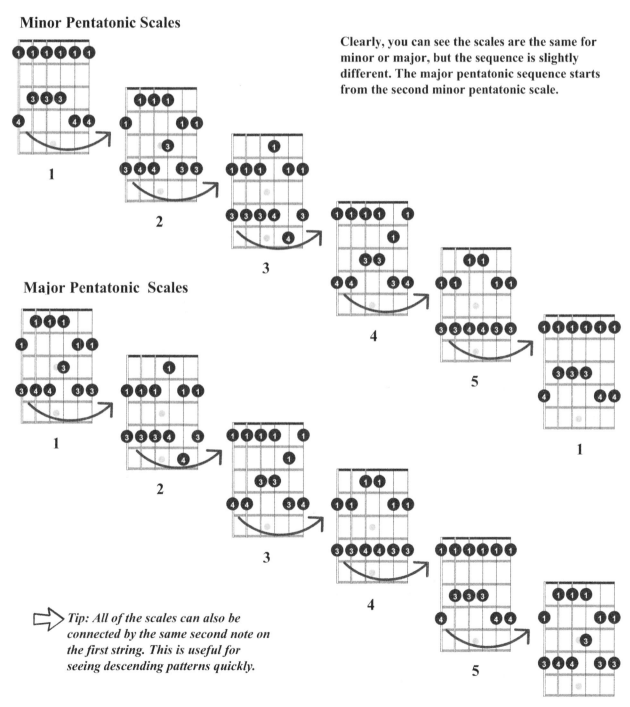

Minor Pentatonic Scales

Clearly, you can see the scales are the same for minor or major, but the sequence is slightly different. The major pentatonic sequence starts from the second minor pentatonic scale.

Major Pentatonic Scales

Tip: All of the scales can also be connected by the same second note on the first string. This is useful for seeing descending patterns quickly.

Connecting Pentatonic Scales III

These diagrams give a little more insight. Play what's shown in the diagrams below by connecting each pentatonic scale to the next and play across all six strings, ascending and descending. You can use the starting fret positions for each scale shown on the diagrams below, or start from any fret connecting the scales the same way.

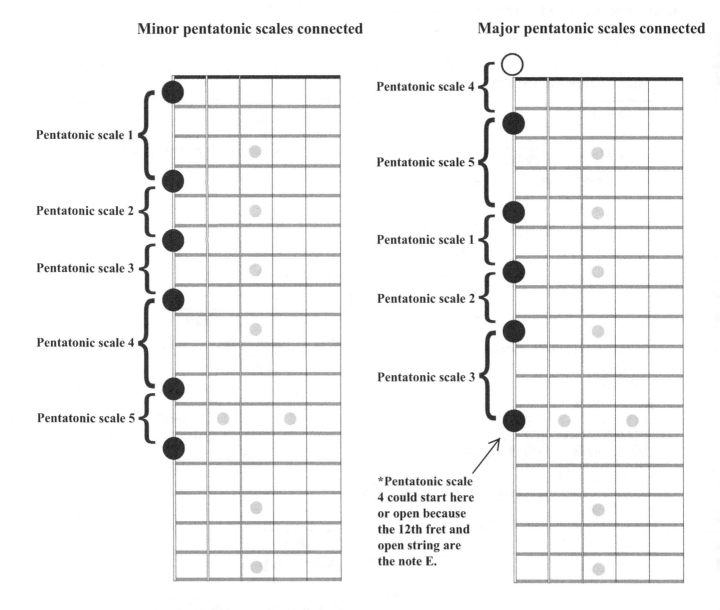

Minor pentatonic scales connected

Pentatonic scale 1

Pentatonic scale 2

Pentatonic scale 3

Pentatonic scale 4

Pentatonic scale 5

Major pentatonic scales connected

Pentatonic scale 4

Pentatonic scale 5

Pentatonic scale 1

Pentatonic scale 2

Pentatonic scale 3

*Pentatonic scale 4 could start here or open because the 12th fret and open string are the note E.

> ⇨ *Tip: Although the above diagrams are labeled minor pentatonic or major pentatonic, their names can be reversed! In the minor pentatonic diagram above, minor pentatonic scale 1 starts on the first fret, which makes all of the other scales in the sequence minor. But the sequence can become major just by starting on the 4th fret with the major pentatonic scale. And the major pentatonic sequence can become minor simply by starting on the second fret with minor pentatonic scale 1.*
>
> *When soloing, you don't have to start with any particular scale to be in major or minor. You can start with any scale that is in the major or minor sequence and even' jump' to another scale within the same sequence.*

Playing in Any Key

A guitarist should have a working knowledge of where the notes are located on the fretboard. If you have learned the notes on the 6th string, you'll be in good shape. But there are ways to find and learn all of the notes on the fretboard! One of which is understanding how the musical alphabet works: **A B C D E F G**, then start over at **A** with sharps and flats in between most of the notes. Understanding where those sharps and flats are on the guitar is essential for finding any note on any string or fret.

Here's an easy summary: Notes in the musical alphabet have a whole step between them, except for B to C and E to F. A whole step skips over a fret. The skipped over fret can be sharp or flat. Because B to C and E to F are half steps, neither a sharp nor a flat can fit between them.

You may call these 'in between' notes by their sharp or flat names. These notes are enharmonic.

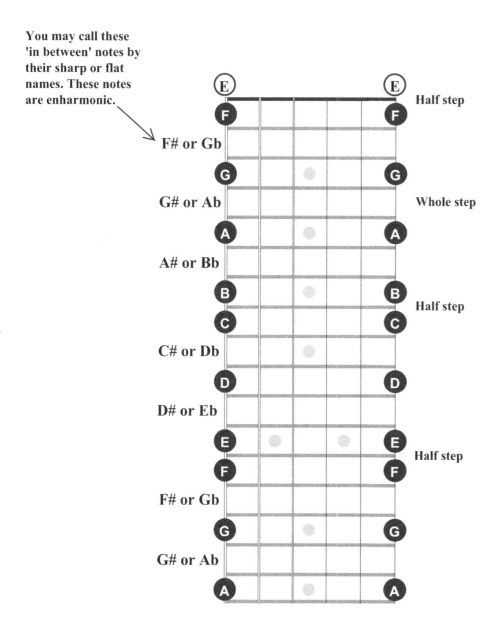

Remember, the notes on the 1st and sixth strings are the same. Recognizing this helps when trying to find notes or keys for descending patterns.

The diagram highlights the half steps between E-F and B-C. Half steps are every fret in succession, and whole steps skip over a fret. Other examples of half steps are F-F# or B-Bb.

Examples of keys and where to start when connecting the scales using notes on the 6th or 1st strings:

Key of G minor

1. Start with minor pentatonic scale 1 on G.

2. Connect minor pentatonic scale 2 which would start from Bb.

3. Now, minor pentatonic scale 3 from C.

4. Minor pentatonic scale 4 from D.

5. Minor pentatonic scale 5 from F.

Key of A major

1. Start with major pentatonic scale 1 on A.

2. Connect major pentatonic scale 2 on a B.

3. Now, major pentatonic scale 3 from a C#.

4. Major pentatonic scale 4 from E.

5. Major pentatonic scale 5 from F#.

Key of E minor

1. Start with minor pentatonic scale 1 on open E or the 12th fret.

2. Connect minor pentatonic scale 2 on a G.

3. Now, minor pentatonic scale 3 from an A.

4. Minor pentatonic scale 4 from B.

5. Minor pentatonic scale 5 from D.

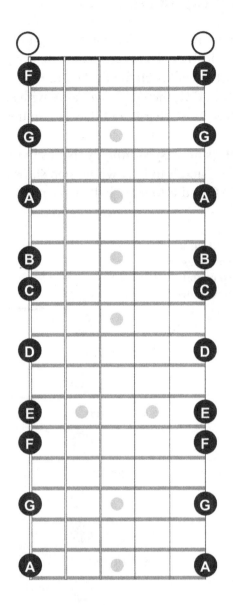

Open E minor pentatonic

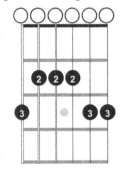

Tip: Each of the keys on this page can be used as a relative major or minor key. In fact, all keys are actually two keys at once. Minor from your first finger, major from your fourth. For example, G minor is also Bb major, or A major is also F# minor, and E minor is also G major.

Scales Within Scales

In pentatonic scale 1 below, look at the fingering that starts the scale: 1-4, 1-3. Locate the same fingering in pentatonic scale 2. This shape contains the same notes and is also the starting point of the fourth string version of minor pentatonic scale 1. This 1-4, 1-3 shape, or fingering, is in all of the scales and can be used to find the beginning of the minor pentatonic scale 1 on different strings. Use the fretboard diagram to help locate minor pentatonic scale 1 on different strings by locating the same note name on different strings. The fretboard diagram will help you see that the notes are the same when the shapes are the same, as long as the scales are in their proper position.

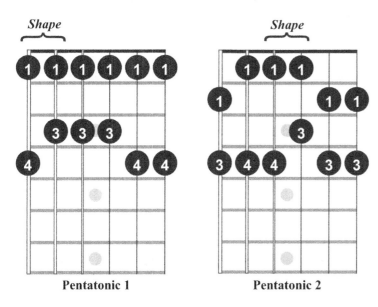

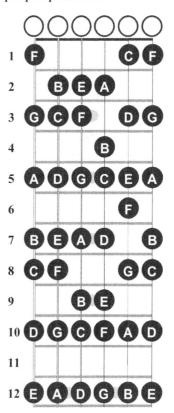

Refer to the above diagrams: Play minor pentatonic scale 1 from A (6th string). Next, connect pentatonic scale 2 from C. Within pentatonic scale 2, pentatonic scale 1 begins from the same recognizable fingering of 1-4, 1-3 starting on the 4th string. Now, play the other scales from their correct positions in the key of A minor and locate the pentatonic scale 1 shape in each of the pentatonic scale patterns shown below.

Notice that the fingerings and notes are the same as long as they are in the same key. The fingering is 1-4, 1-3 in all of the examples below, and the notes are A, C, D, and E.

Key of A minor

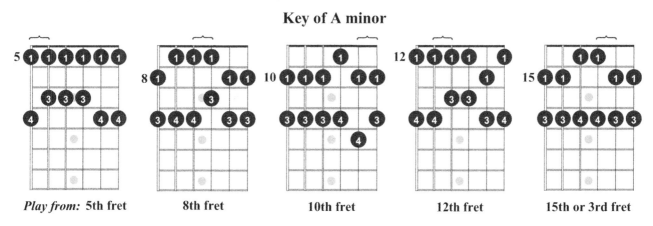

Play from: **5th fret**   **8th fret**   **10th fret**   **12th fret**   **15th or 3rd fret**

Using Shapes to Find Roots

Each scale has two shapes that can be used as visual cues to quickly find the major or minor roots within each scale. We can see the minor pentatonic scale 1 in every other scale, easily identified by the fingering 1-4, 1-3 shape as shown on the previous page.

Remember the 1-4 fingering that begins minor pentatonic scale 1 can be used to think of the scale as major or minor. Use the 1st finger to determine the root of a minor key and the 4th finger to determine the root of a major key.

Now look for this fingering 1-3, 1-3, 1-3 in the diagrams below. Easy to spot! Within this group of notes lie the roots of major and minor.

The line connecting 3-1 illustrates another shape used to identify major or minor roots within the pentatonic scales. In each diagram, finger 3 represents the minor pentatonic root and finger 1 the major pentatonic root.

*1-3, 1-3, 1-3 shape shown under the brackets.

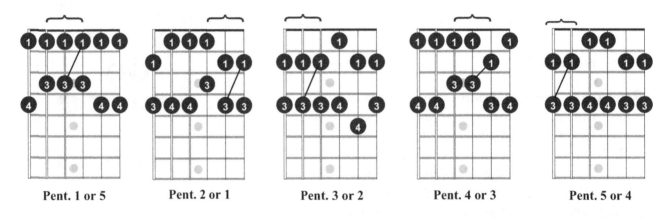

| Pent. 1 or 5 | Pent. 2 or 1 | Pent. 3 or 2 | Pent. 4 or 3 | Pent. 5 or 4 |

*1-3, 1-3, 1-3 fingering wraps around in this scale.

*Reminder: your 1st and 6th strings on the guitar are both called E. Any roots found on the 6th string will also be found on the 1st string.

Pentatonics from any String

Any of the 5 pentatonic scales can be played starting from any string. This is very easy to figure out simply by looking at each scale's original fingering or shape. Being able to spot these fingerings and shapes within each scale helps a guitarist find other places on the fretboard quickly by starting on any string, which makes it easy to jump to new positions while soloing, so you don't have to rely only on connecting from the 6th or 1st strings.

Minor pentatonic scale 1 fingering is: 1-4, 1-3, 1-3, 1-3, 1-4, 1-4. This fingering is repeated within all of the other scales. This is because all of the scales are based on the same group of notes, and **all five pentatonic scales, whether you call them major or minor, are all just one big pentatonic scale!**

Look at the large pentatonic scale 1 diagram below and notice the numbers above the strings. The numbers represent the starting string for each of the pentatonic scales from within the larger pattern. The starting strings for each of the pentatonic scales are shown in the smaller diagrams below.

Try this:

Start with pentatonic 1 at the 5th fret (key of Am), but start by playing from the 5th string, which is pentatonic scale 3, shown in the first smaller diagram below. Now, play the larger pentatonic scale 3 from its position in this key (10th fret). Notice that the notes are the same for both scales.

Pentatonic 1

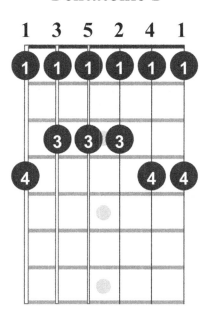

*Keep in mind the notes on the sixth and first strings are the same.

Pentatonic scales starting from different strings within minor pentatonic scale 1.

Pentatonic 3   Pentatonic 5

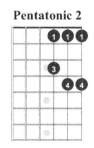

Pentatonic 2   Pentatonic 4

Pentatonic 1 or 5

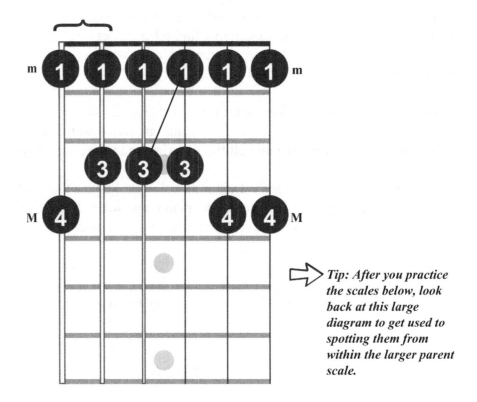

Reminder: Within the bracket, finger 1 represents the minor root, fingering 4 the major root.

3-1 with the connecting line; 3 represents the minor root and 1 the major root.

Tip: *After you practice the scales below, look back at this large diagram to get used to spotting them from within the larger parent scale.*

Play through the shapes below, ascending and descending. As you are playing, think of where the roots are for major and minor within each of the shapes.

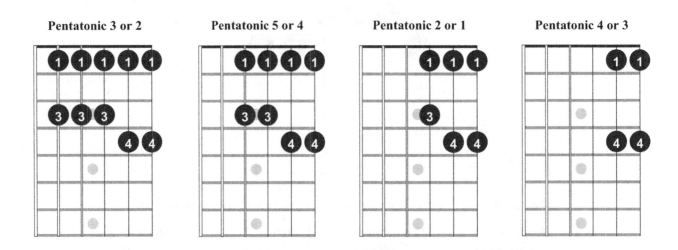

Pentatonic 3 or 2   **Pentatonic 5 or 4**   **Pentatonic 2 or 1**   **Pentatonic 4 or 3**

*These smaller scale shapes should be practiced individually. They can be played from any fret, but it is best to practice them from their correct position in key.

Pentatonic 2 or 1

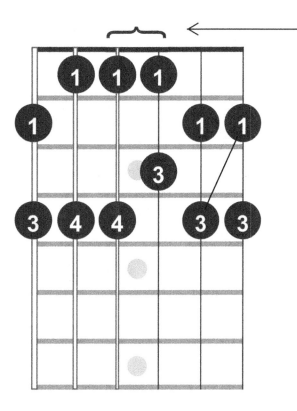

This bracket is only here to make the 1-4 and 1-3 fingering easy to spot throughout the scales. The 1-4 fingering within this group is all we need to determine the minor or major root.

Play through the shapes below, ascending and descending. As you are playing, think of where the roots are for major and minor within each of the shapes.

Pentatonic 4 or 3   **Pentatonic 1 or 5**   **Pentatonic 3 or 2**   **Pentatonic 5 or 4**

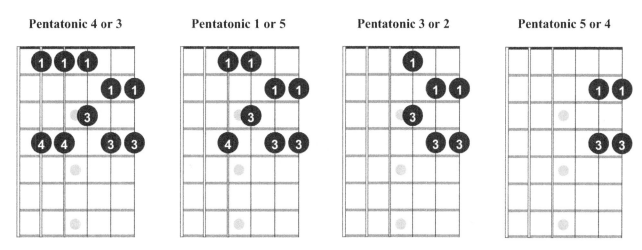

Pentatonic 3 or 2

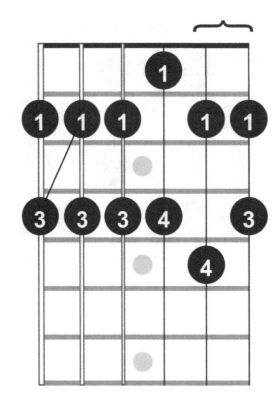

Reminder: Within the bracket, finger 1 represents the minor root, finger 4 the major root.

The 3-1 with the connecting line: 3 represents the minor root and 1 the major root.

Play through the shapes below, ascending and descending. As you are playing, think of where the roots are for major and minor within each of the shapes.

Pentatonic 5 or 4 **Pentatonic 2 or 1** **Pentatonic 4 or 3** **Pentatonic 1 or 5**

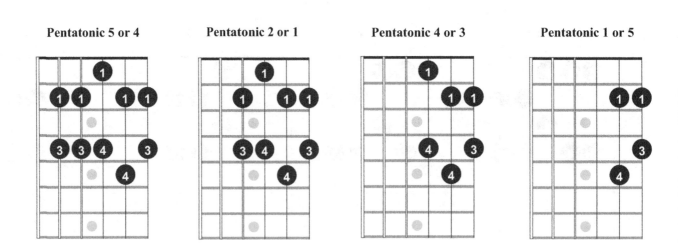

Pentatonic 4 or 3

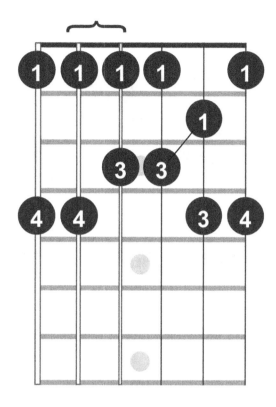

Play through the shapes below, ascending and descending. As you are playing, think of where the roots are for major and minor within each of the shapes.

Pentatonic 1 or 5   Pentatonic 3 or 2   Pentatonic 5 or 4   Pentatonic 2 or 1

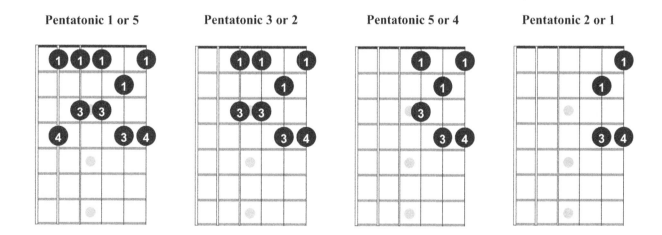

Pentatonic 5 or 4

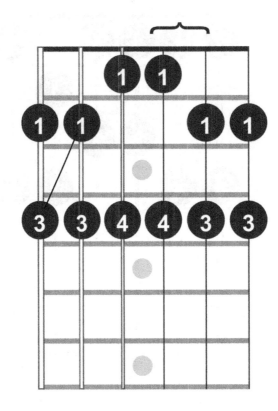

Play through the shapes below, ascending and descending. As you are playing, think of where the roots are for major and minor within each of the shapes.

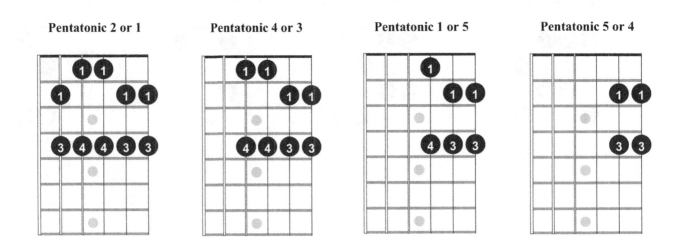

Pentatonic 2 or 1   Pentatonic 4 or 3   Pentatonic 1 or 5   Pentatonic 5 or 4

Pentatonic Scales 1 & 2 Connected Patterns

These exercises on the next pages combine pentatonic scales by shifting back and forth between two scales at a time. The minor pentatonic scale numbering sequence will be used. Ascending and descending should be practiced as separate examples. The examples are in the key of A minor or C major, which is a comfortable place to start. Once you get used to an exercise, move it to another key.

Practice these two scales with alternate picking, then with hammer-ons and pull-offs, ascending and descending, before proceeding to the next section. Pentatonic scale 1 from the 5th fret and pentatonic scale 2 from the 8th fret.

Pentatonic Scale 1

Pentatonic scale 2

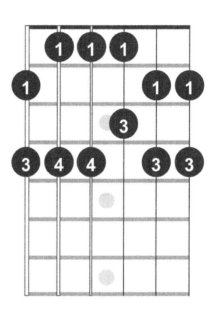

Tip: When shifting between scales, the original fingerings will work well, but you may find small sections where the alternate fingerings work better for you. If you practiced the scales well with their alternate fingerings earlier in this book, then the fingerings in the upcoming exercises will be easy to figure out.

In each example, pentatonic 1 starts with frets 5-8 and pentatonic 2 starts with 8-10.

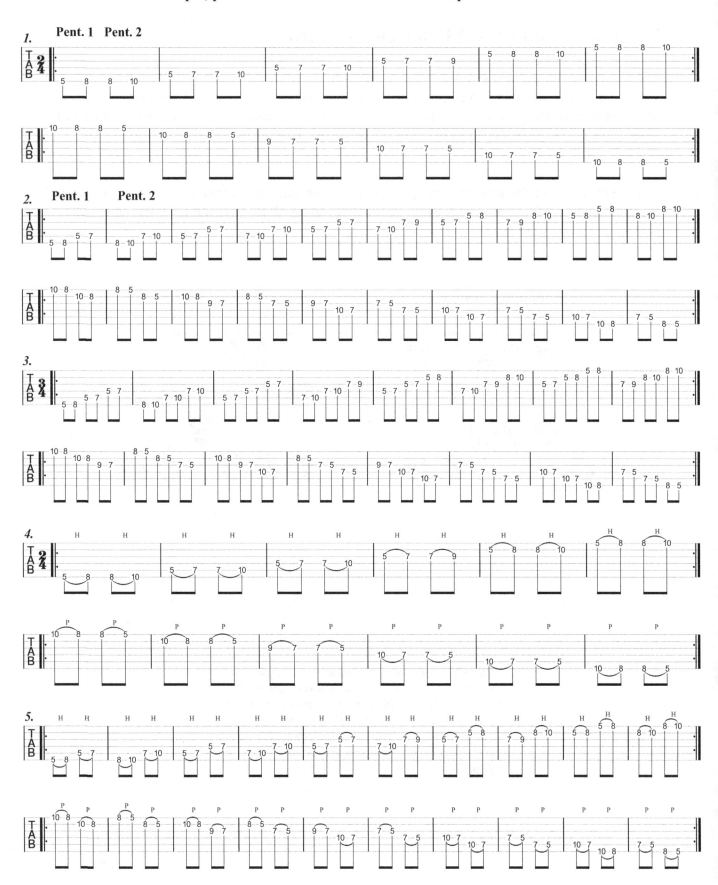

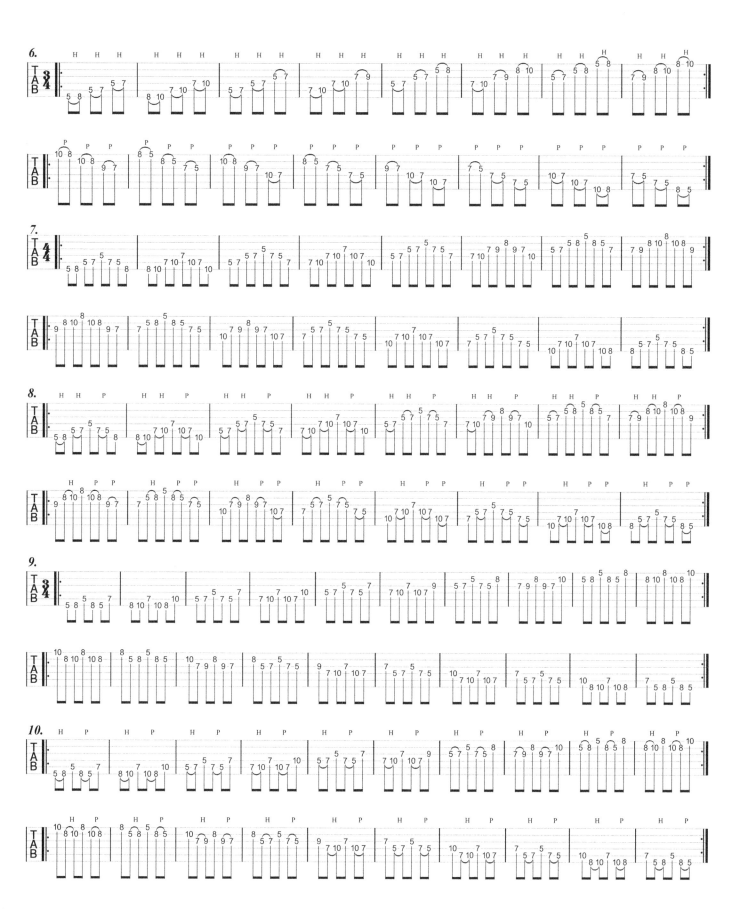

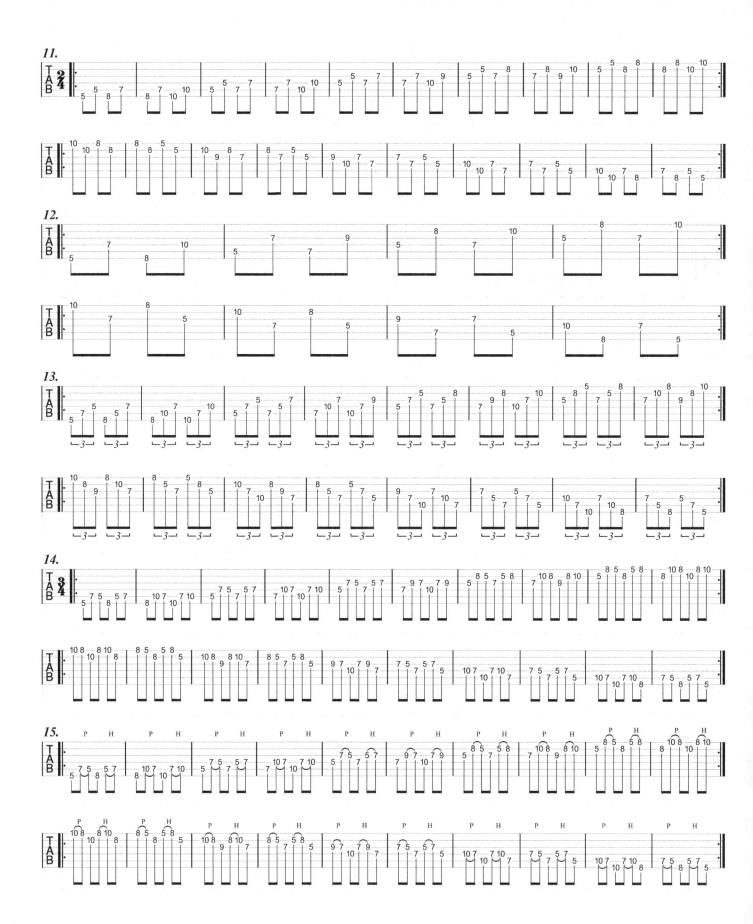

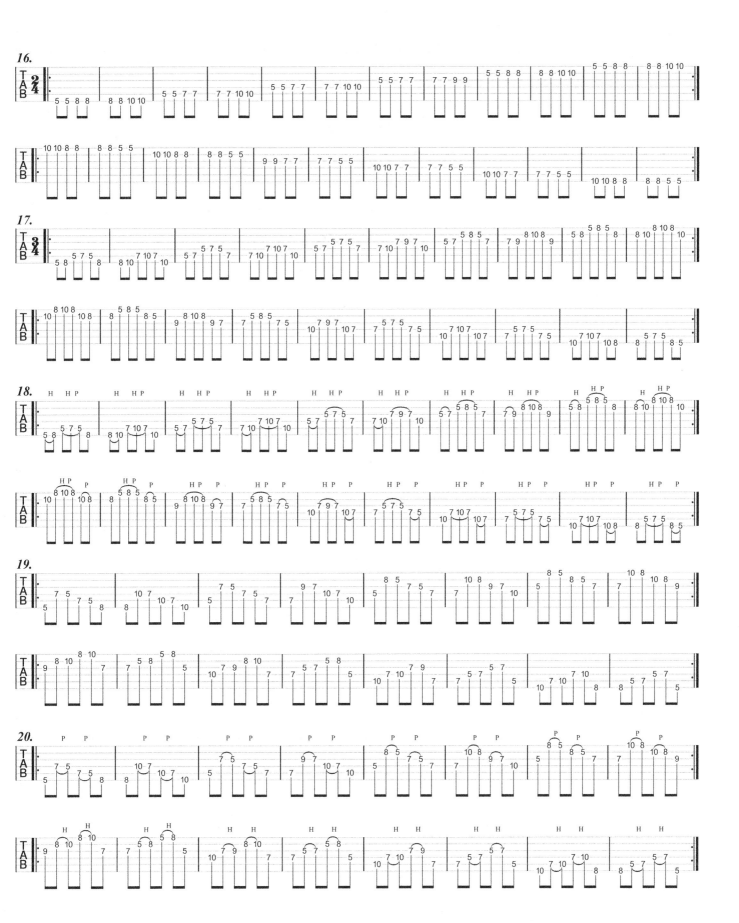

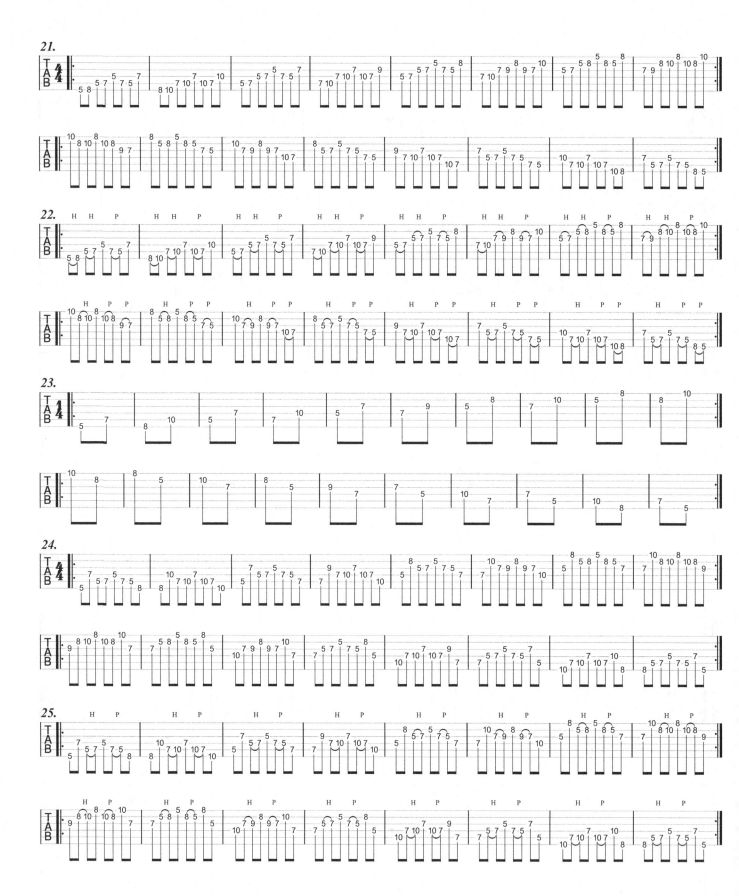

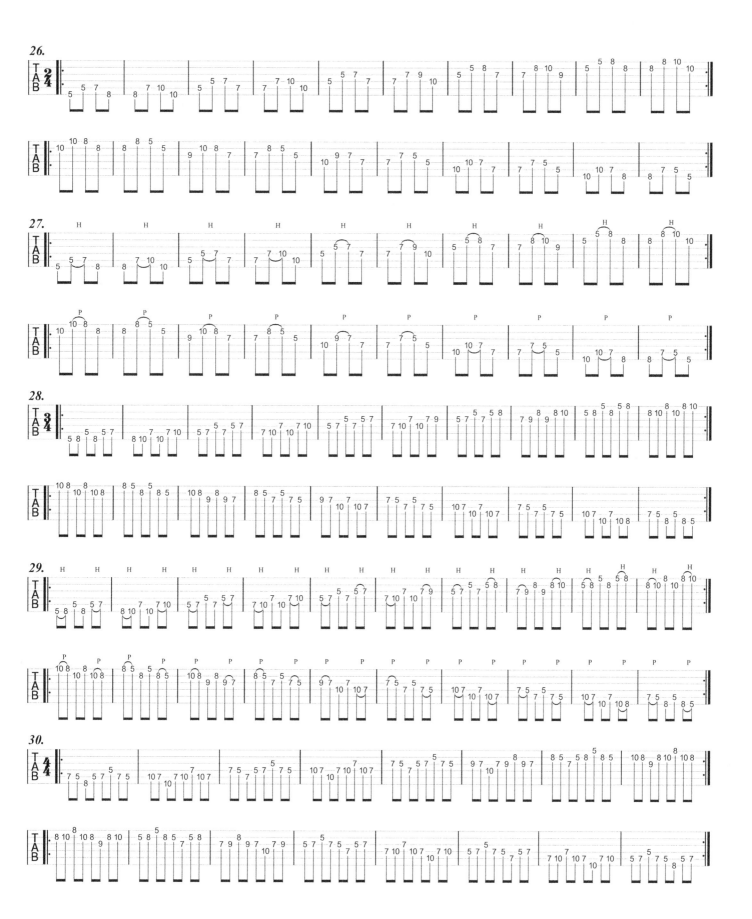

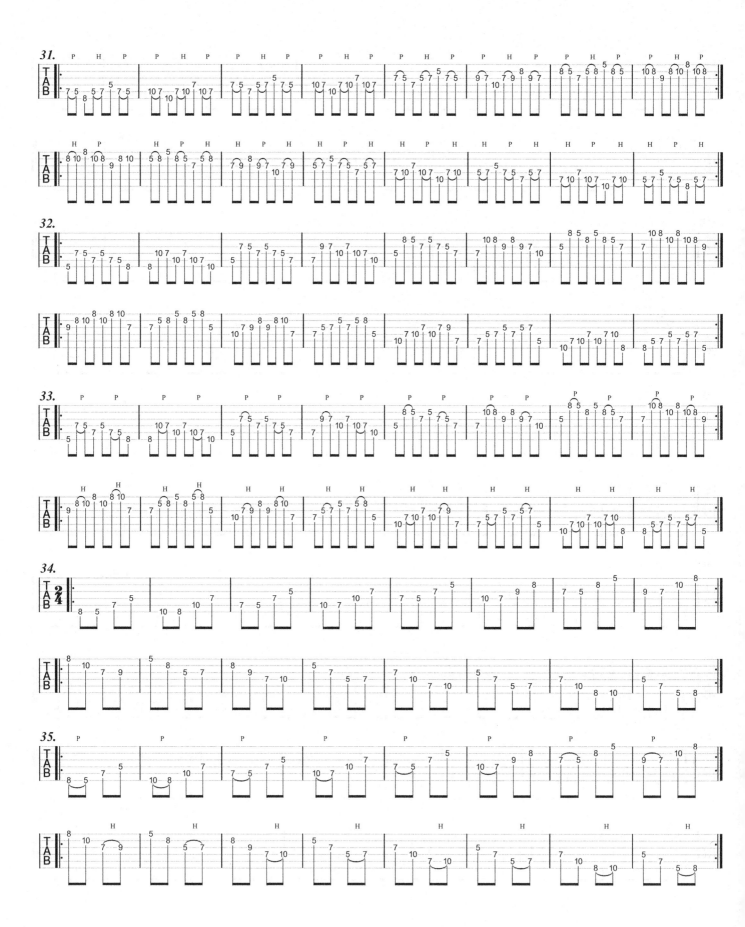

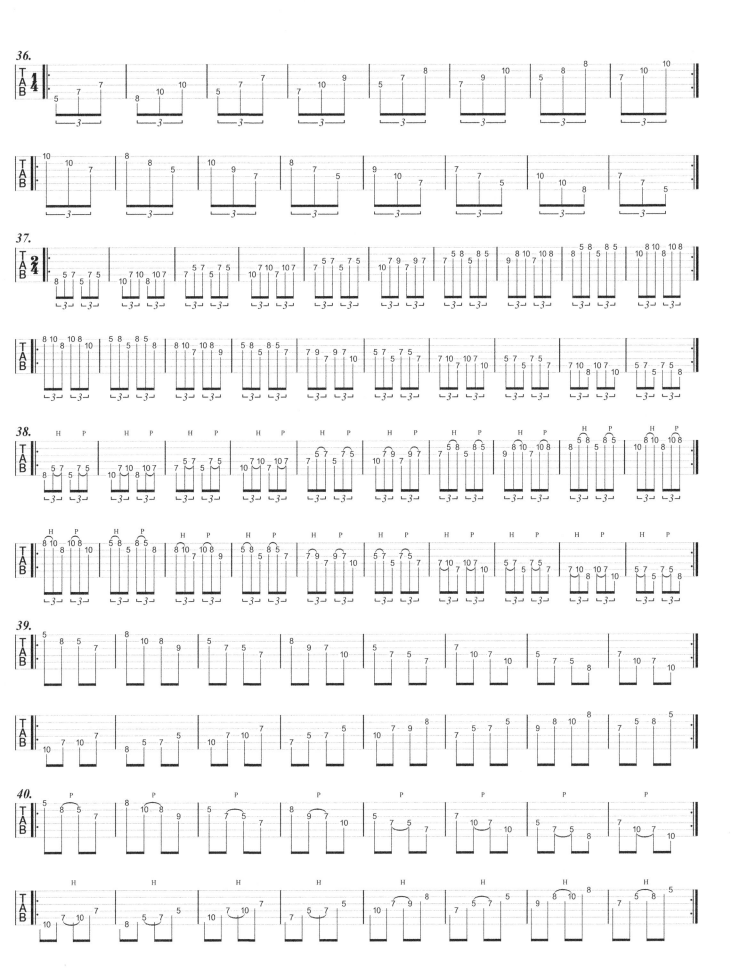

41.

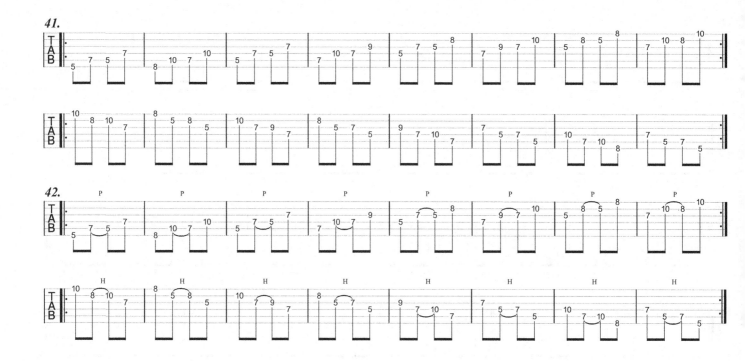

Pentatonic Scales 2 & 3 Connected Patterns

Practice these two scales with alternate picking, then with hammer-ons and pull-offs, ascending and descending, before proceeding to the next section. Pentatonic scale 2 from the 8th fret and pentatonic scale 3 from the 10th fret.

Pentatonic scale 2   **Pentatonic scale 3**

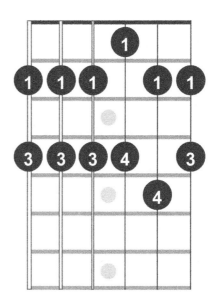

In each example, pentatonic 2 starts with frets 8-10 and pentatonic 3 starts with 10-12.

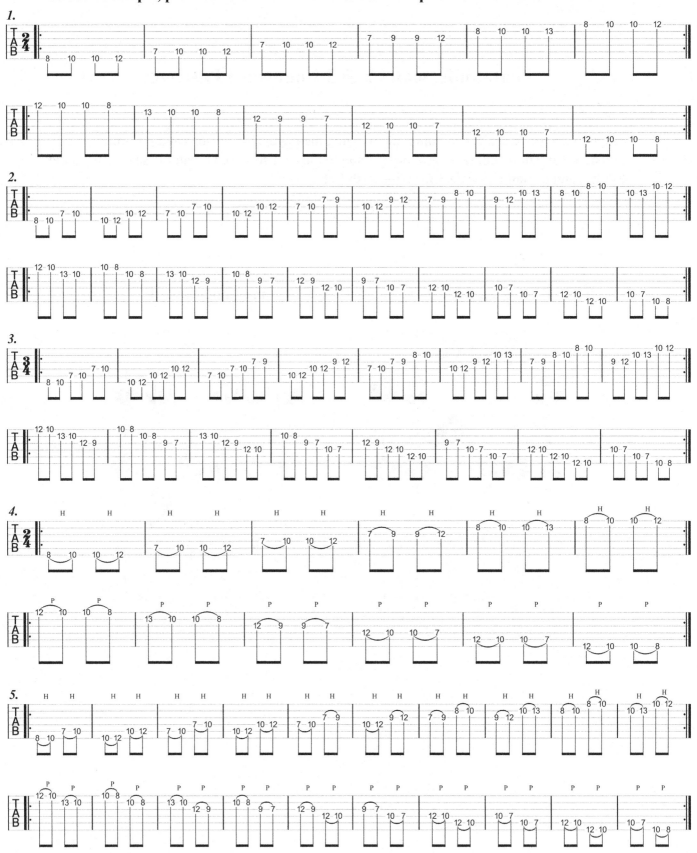

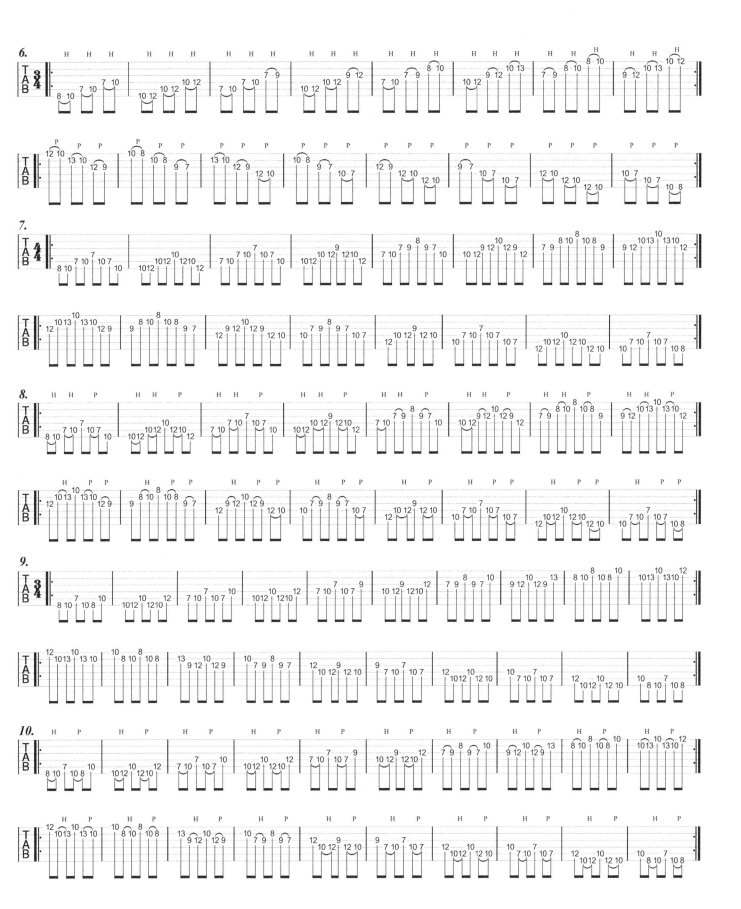

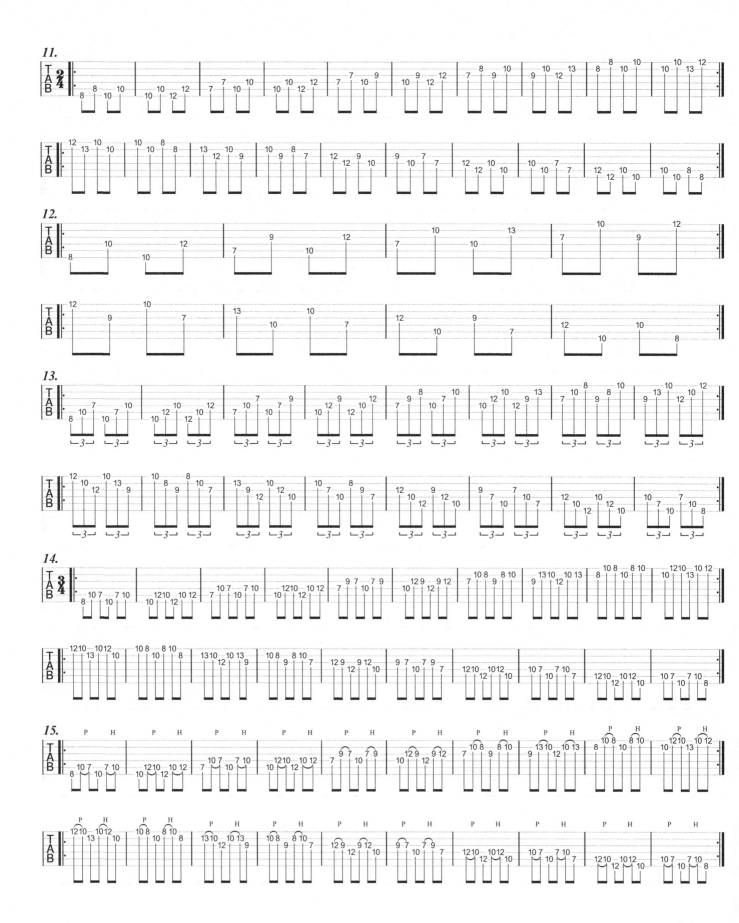

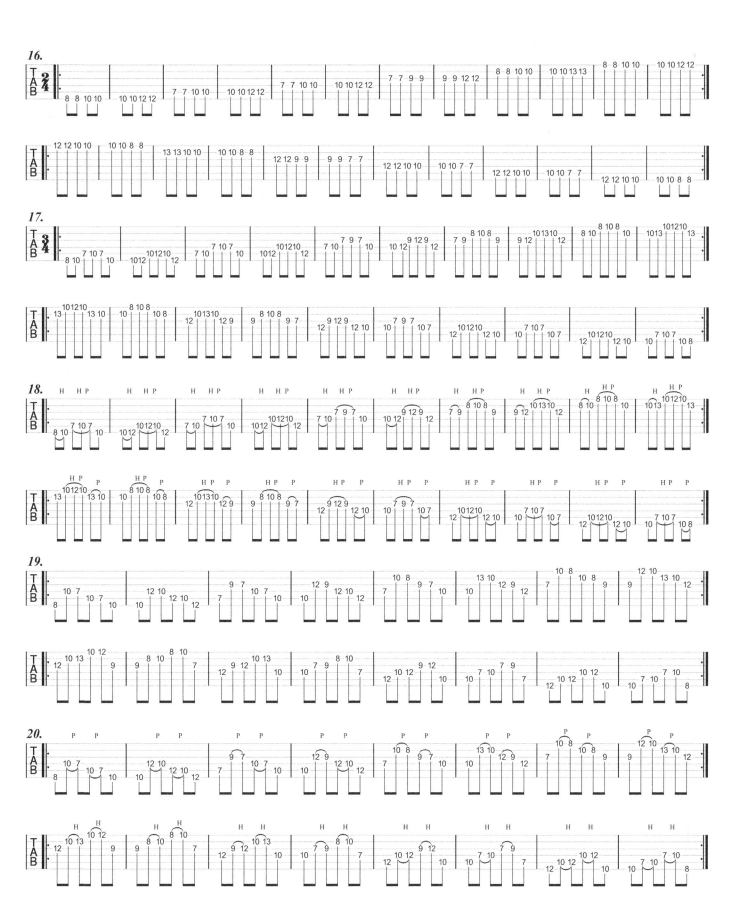

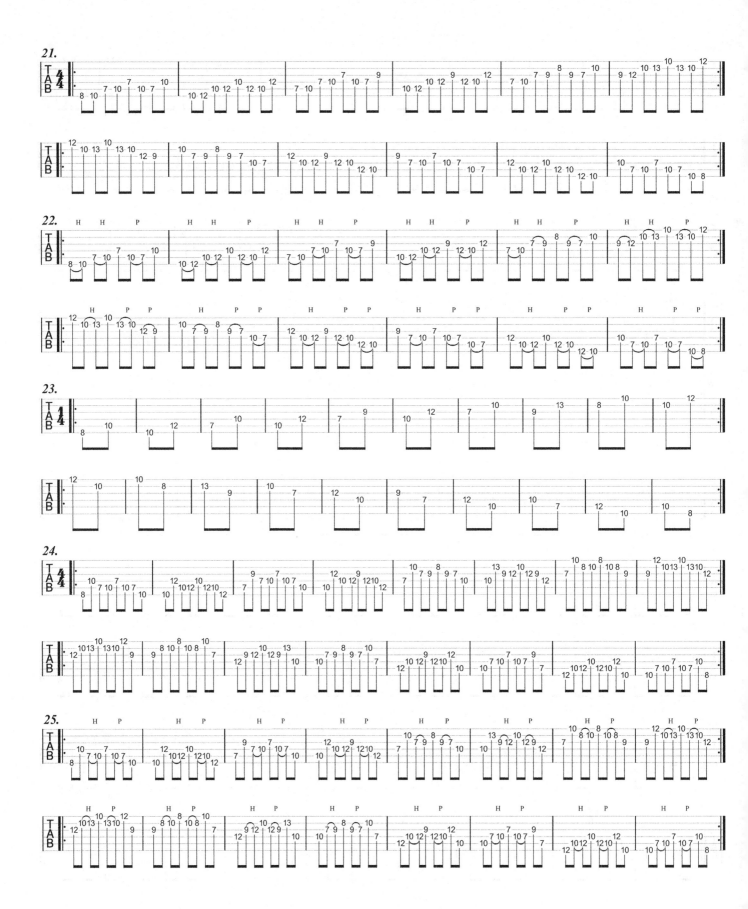

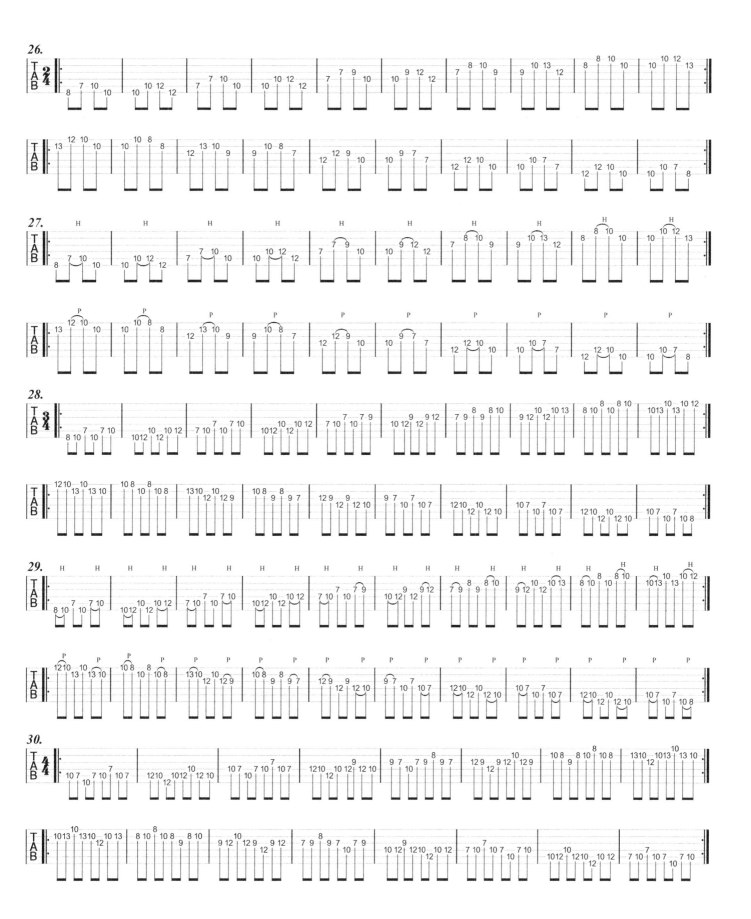

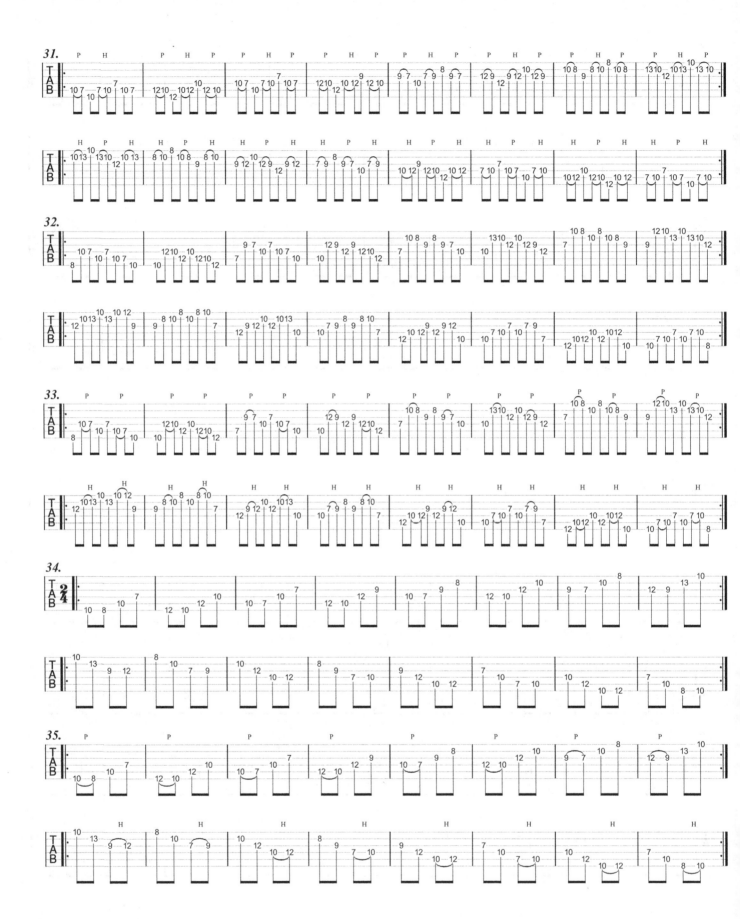

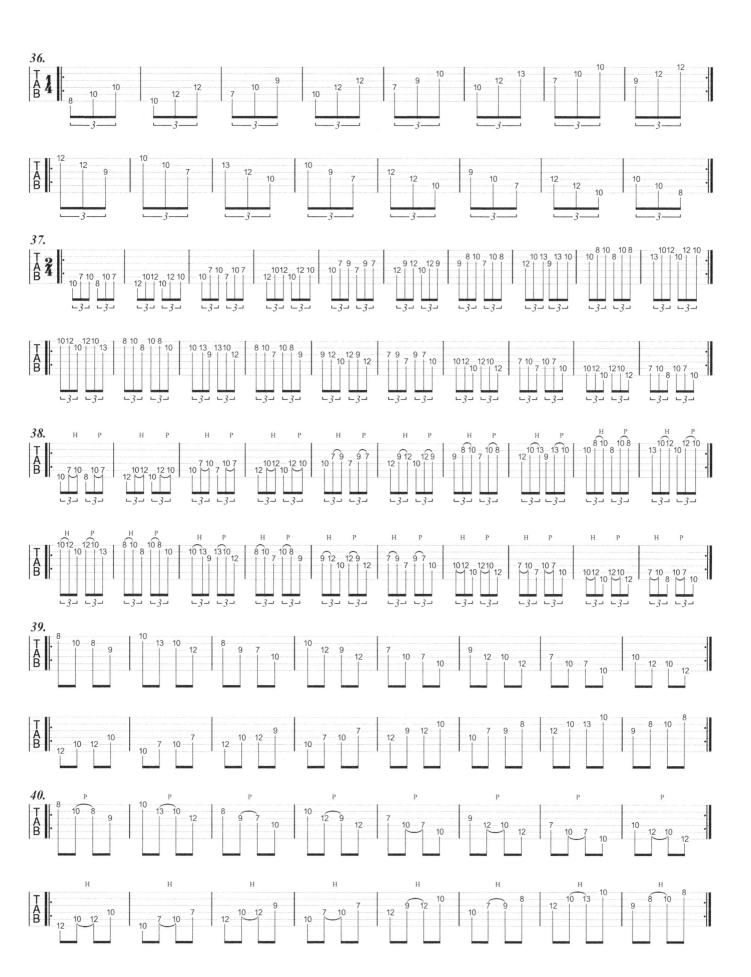

41.

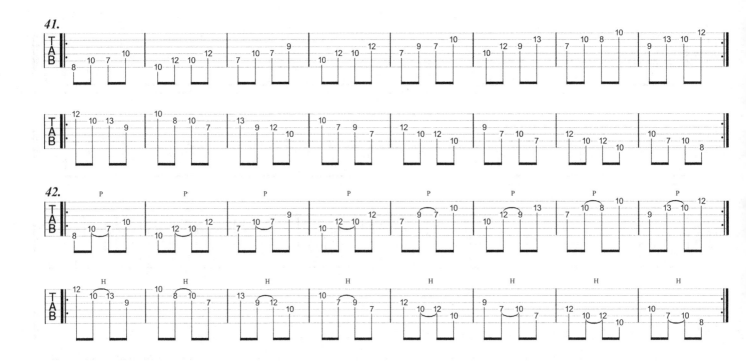

42.

Pentatonic Scales 3 & 4 Connected Patterns

Practice these two scales with alternate picking, then with hammer-ons and pull-offs, ascending and descending, before proceeding to the next section. Pentatonic scale 3 from the 10th fret and pentatonic scale 4 from the 12th fret.

Pentatonic scale 3

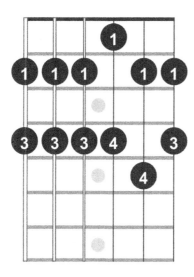

Pentatonic scale 4

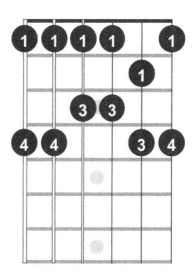

In each example, pentatonic 3 starts with frets 10-12 and pentatonic 4 starts with 12-15.

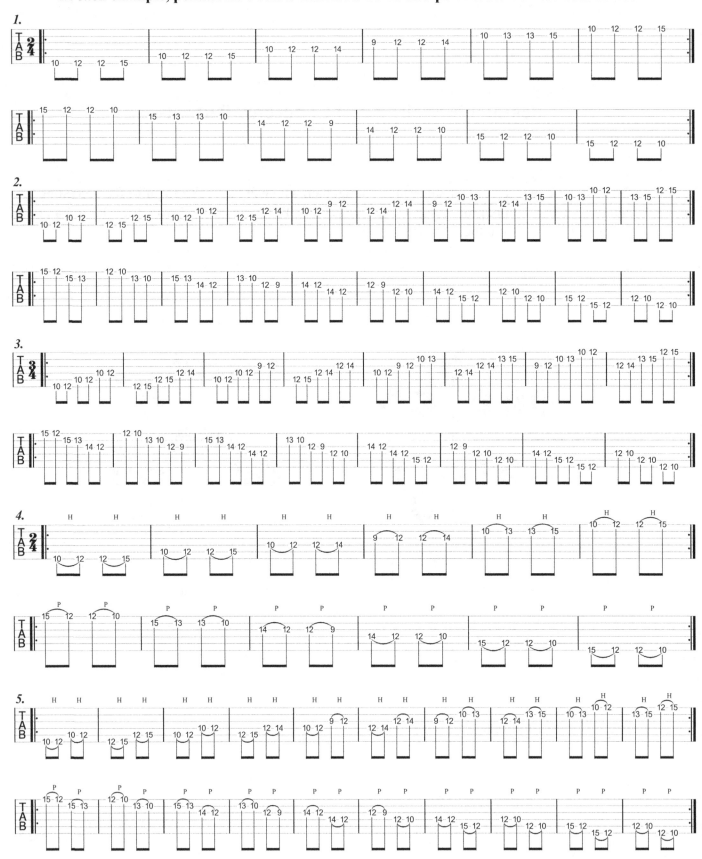

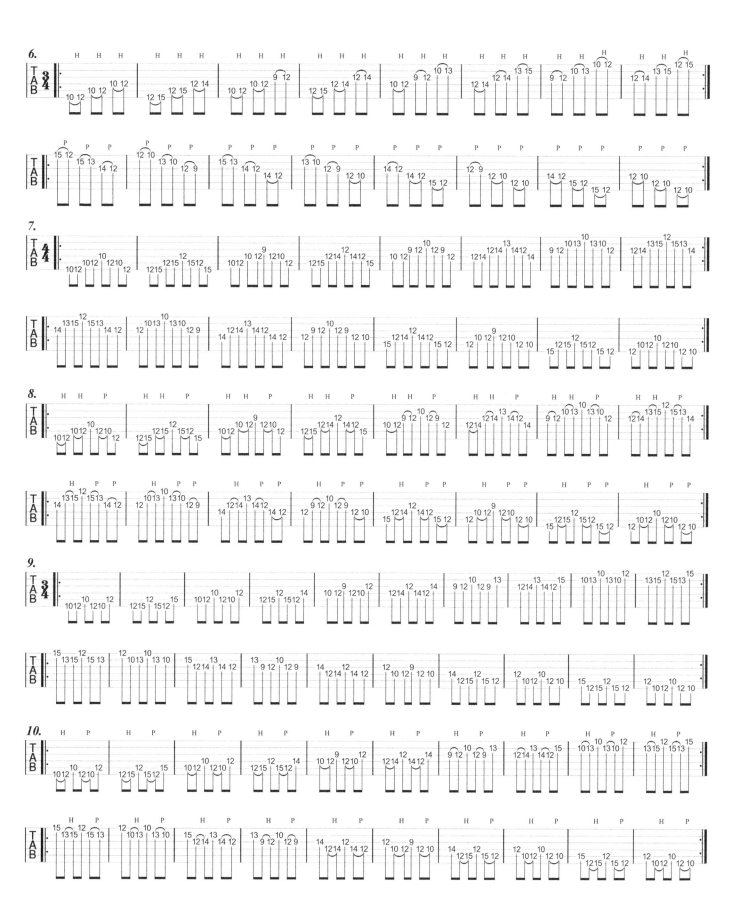

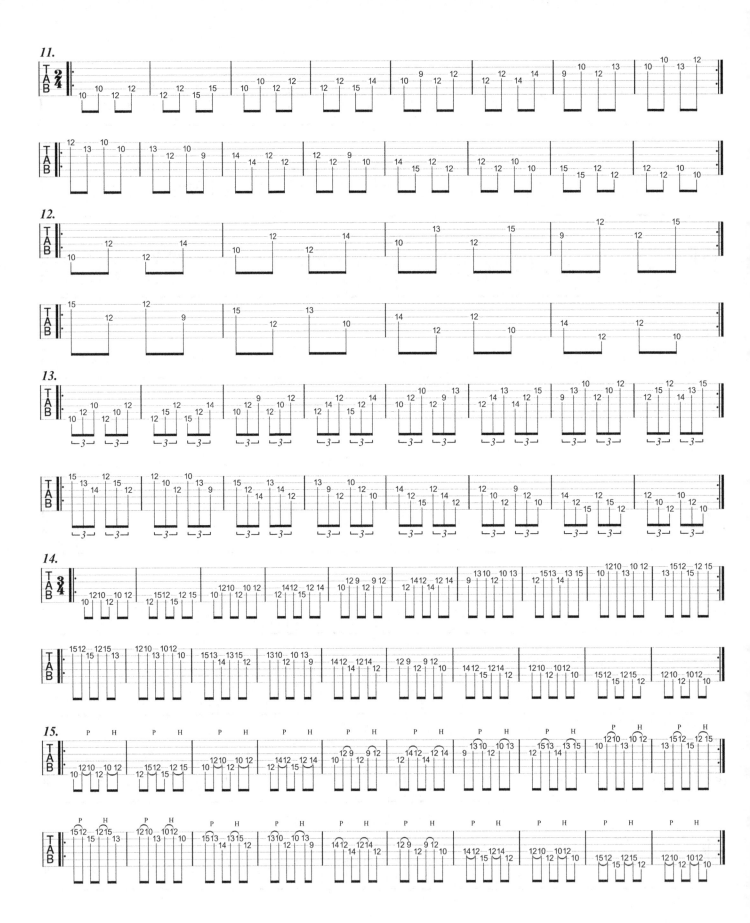

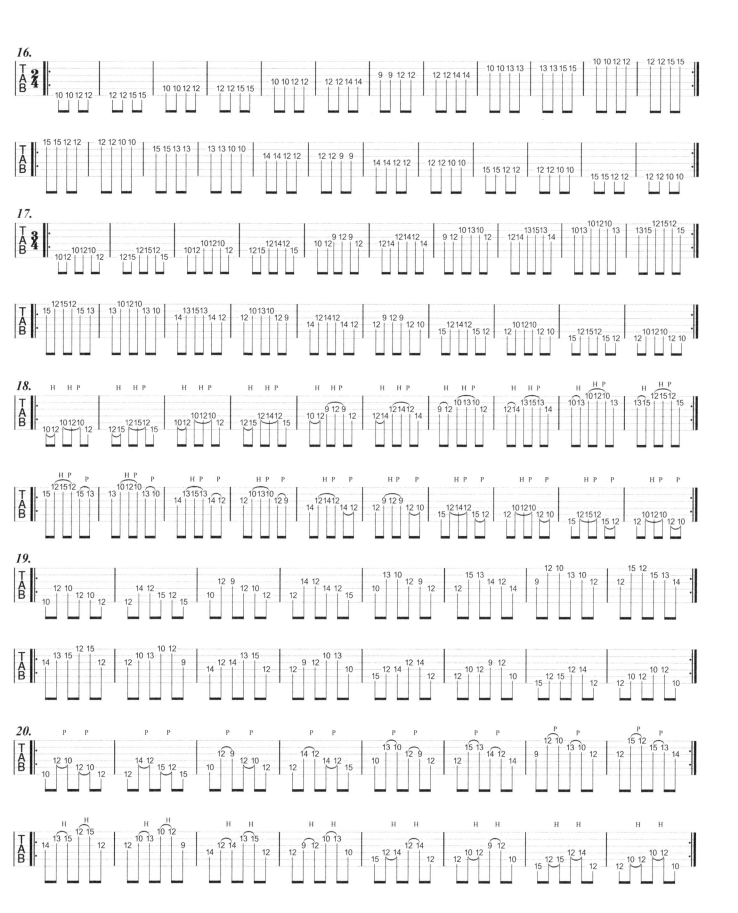

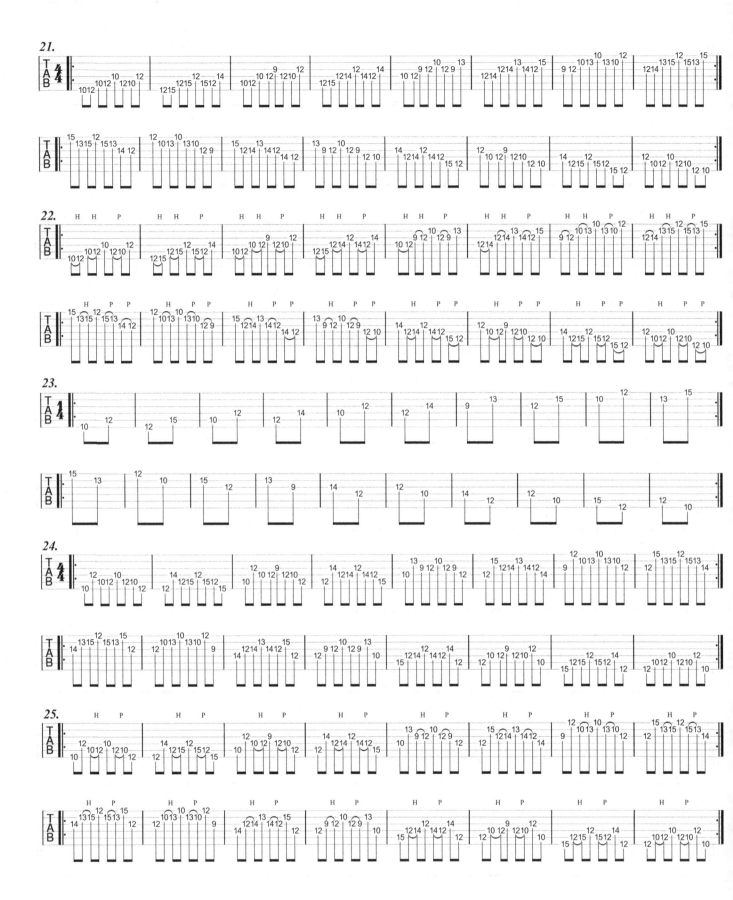

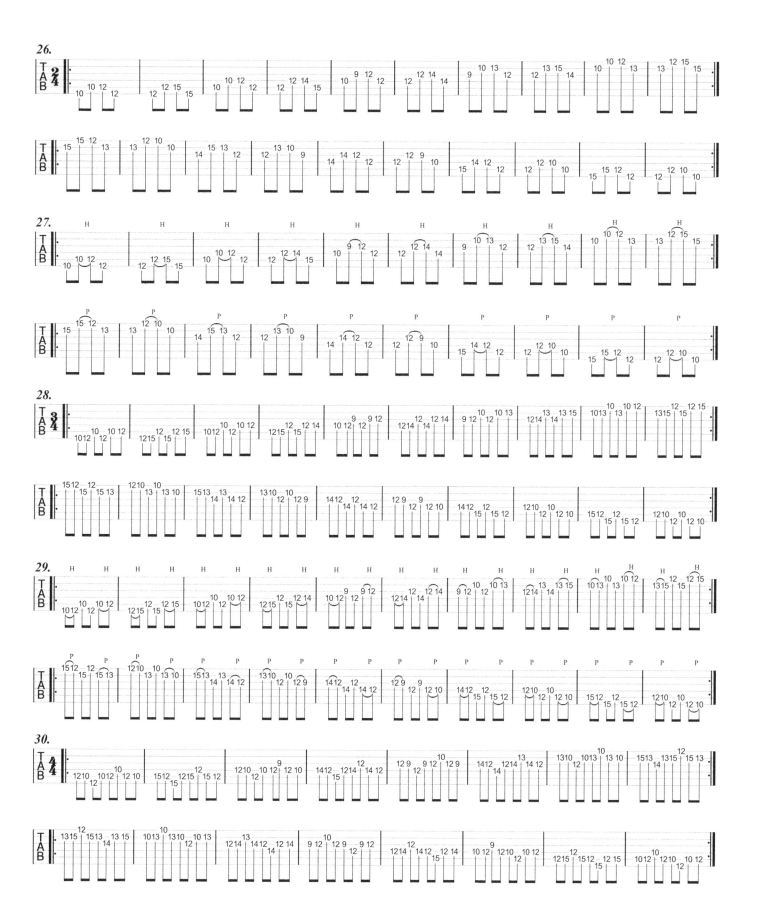

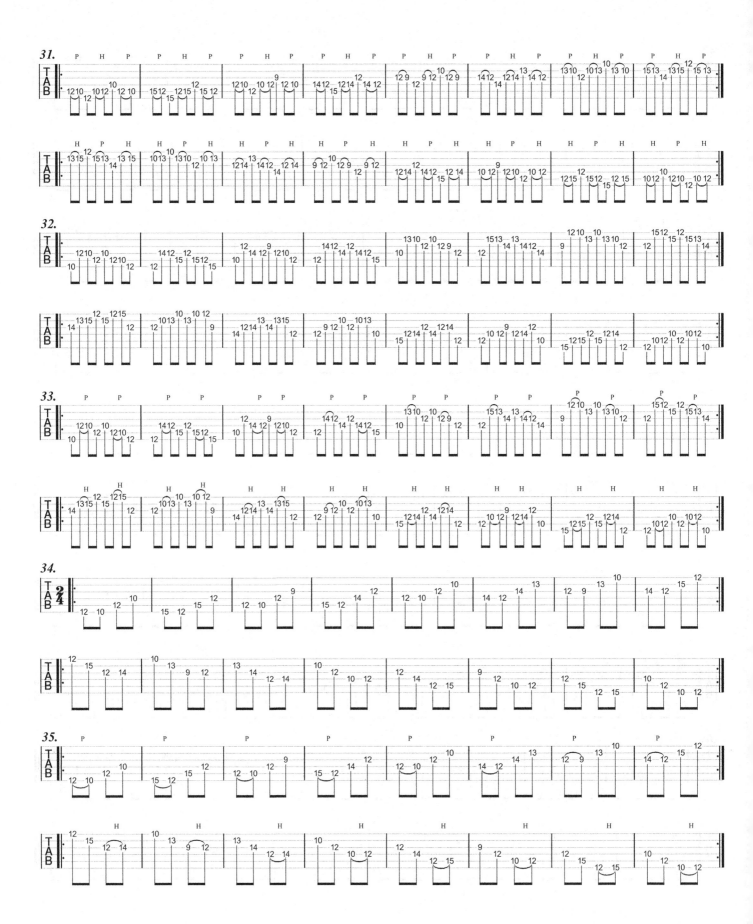

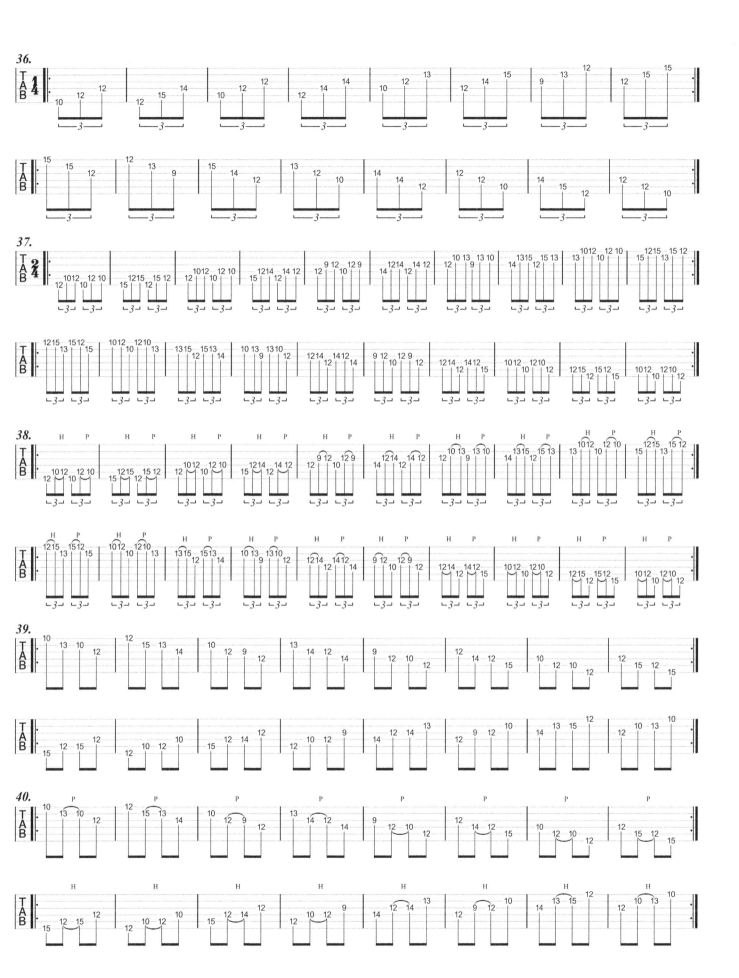

41.

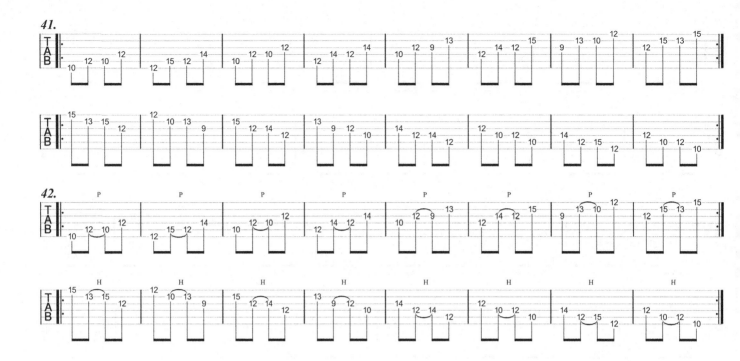

42.

Pentatonic Scales 4 & 5 Connected Patterns

Practice these two scales with alternate picking, then with hammer-ons and pull-offs, ascending and descending, before proceeding to the next section. Pentatonic scale 4, from the 12th fret, and pentatonic scale 5, from the 15th fret.

Pentatonic scale 4   ### Pentatonic scale 5

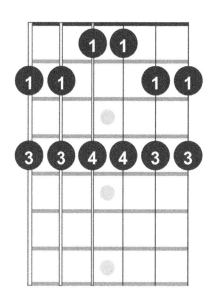

In each example, pentatonic 4 starts with frets 12-15 and pentatonic 5 starts with 15-17.

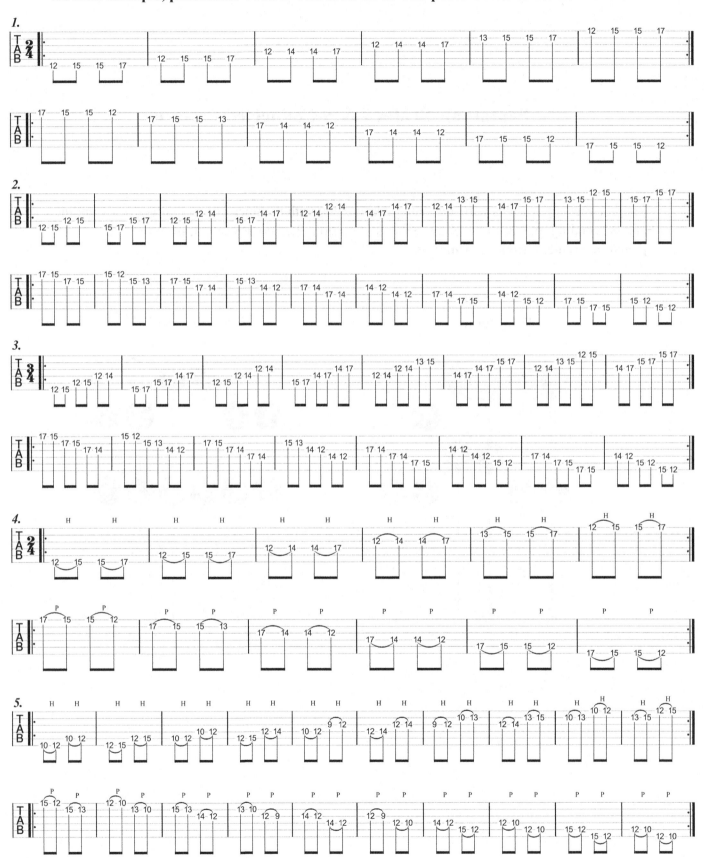

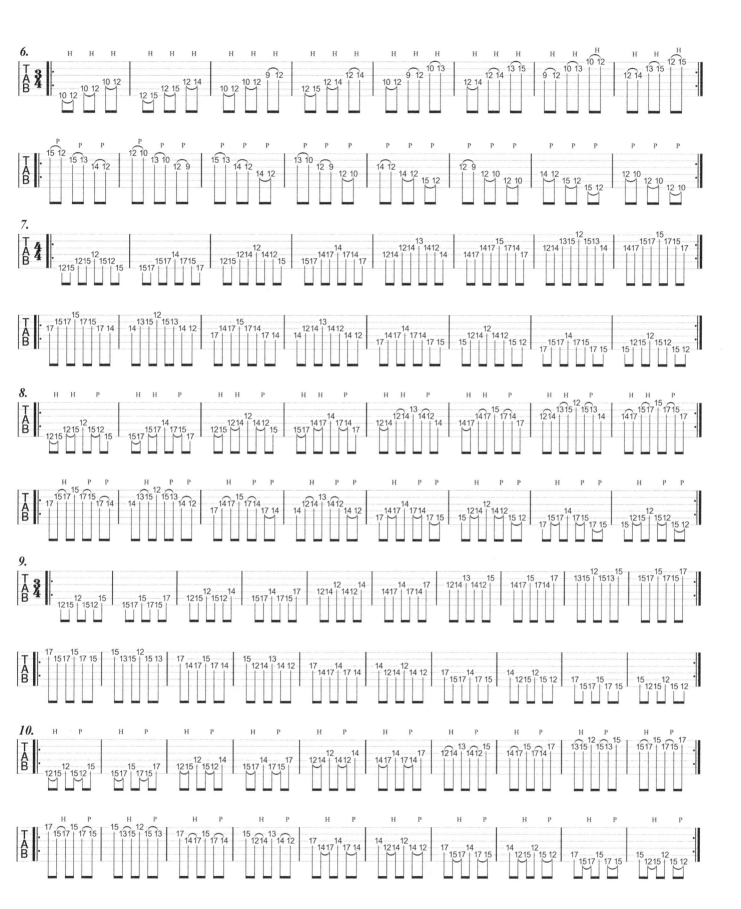

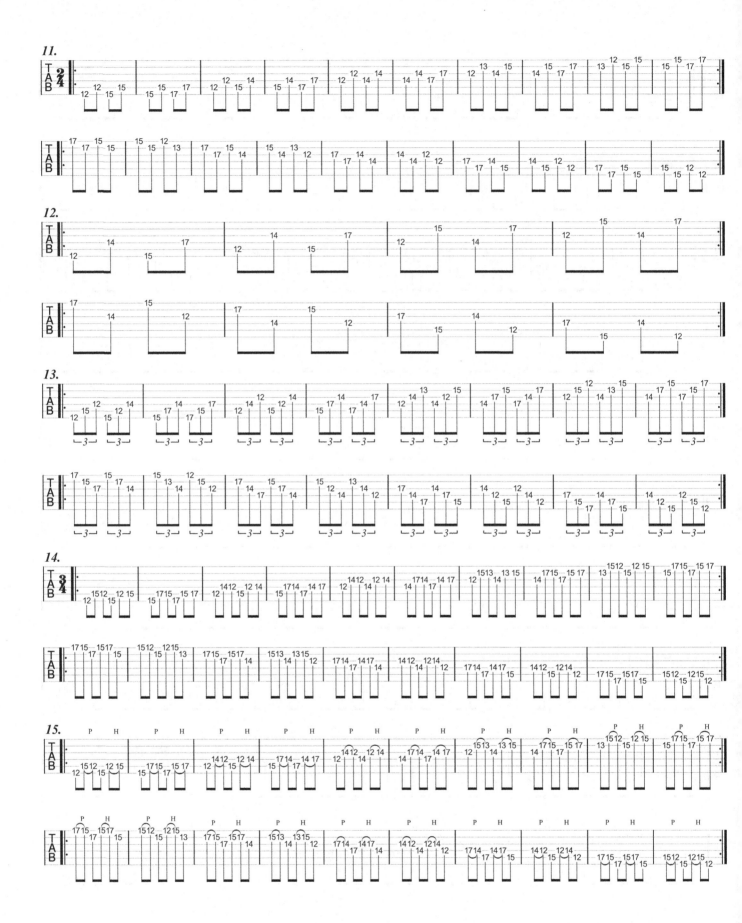

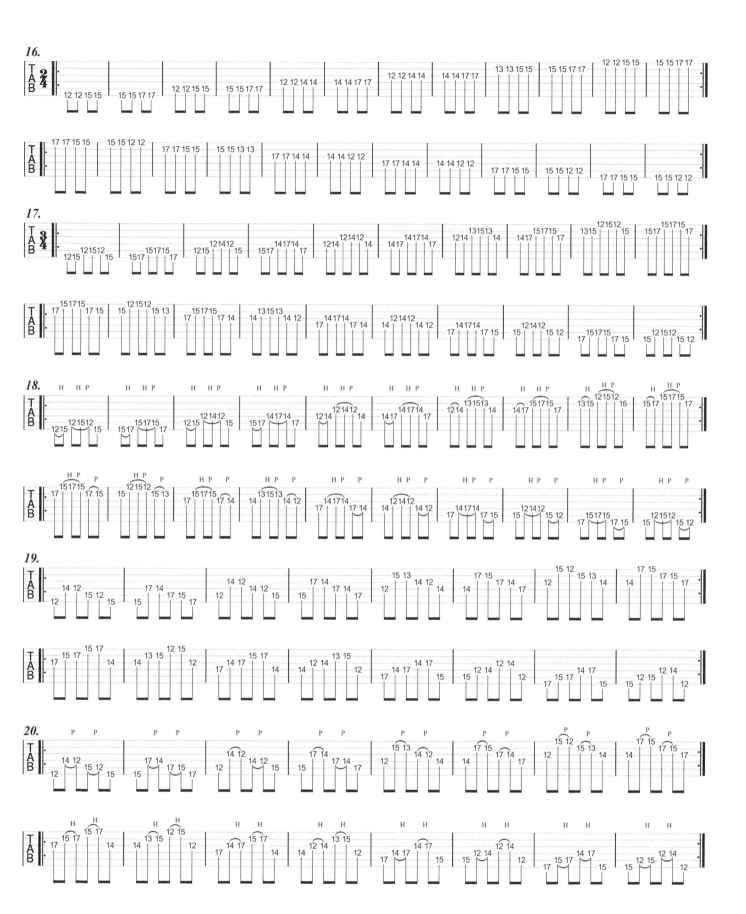

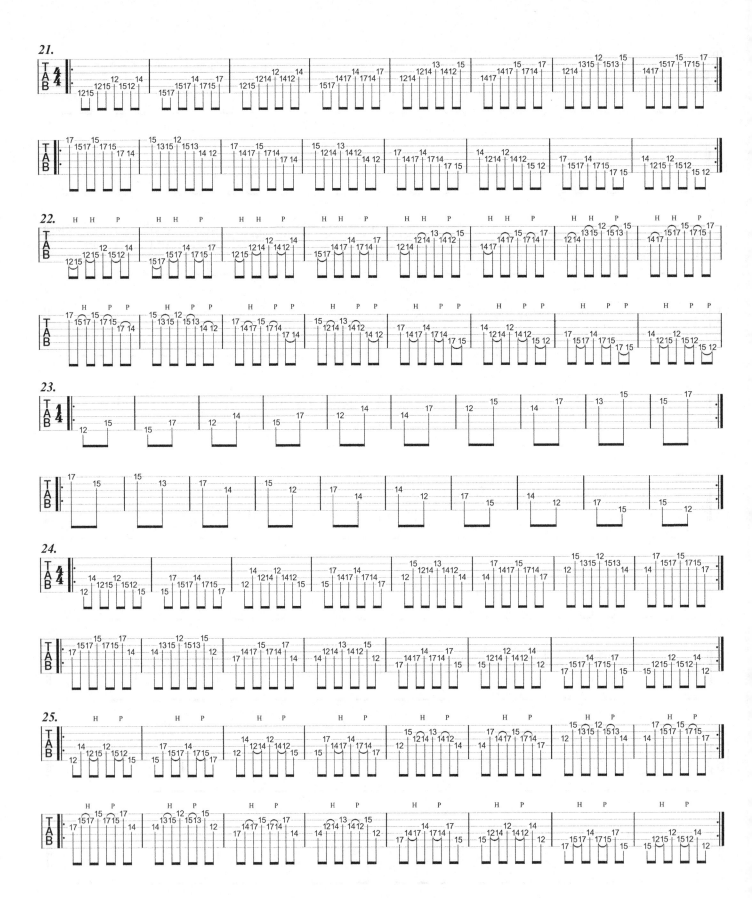

100

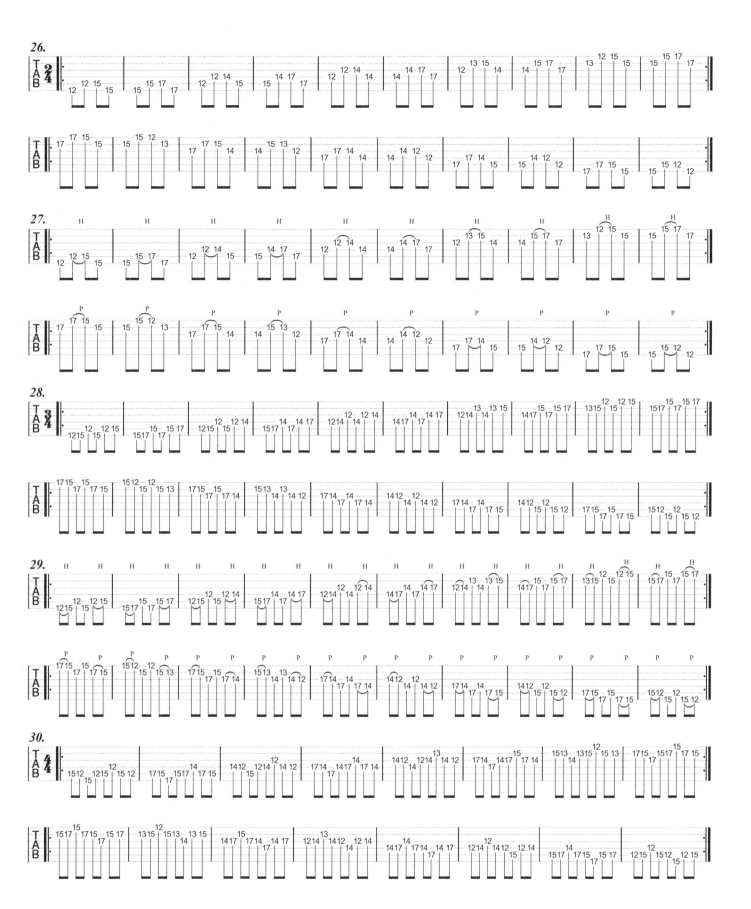

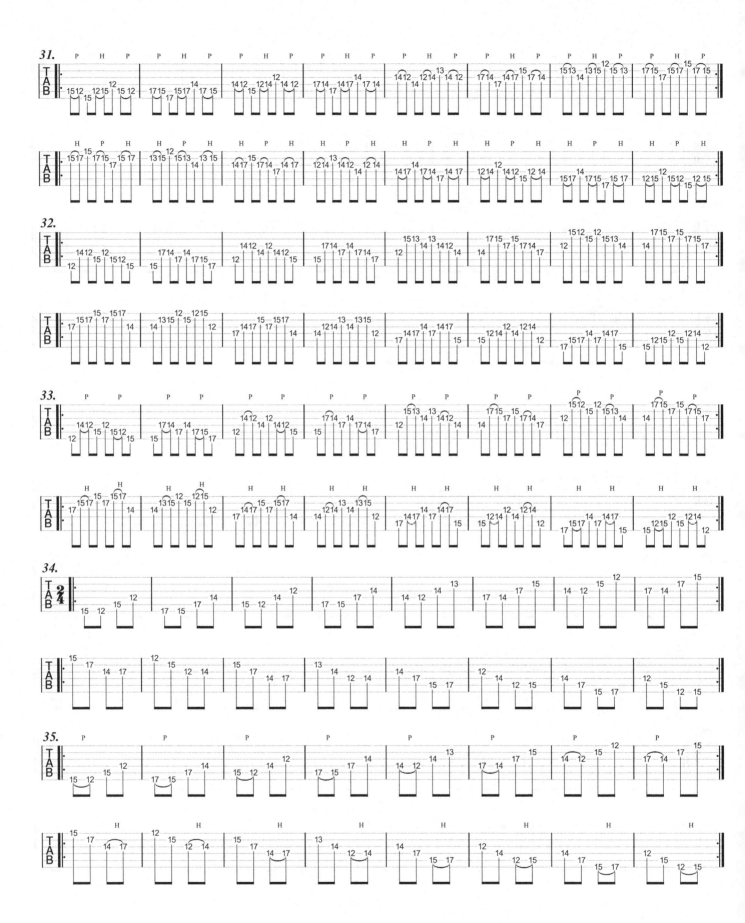

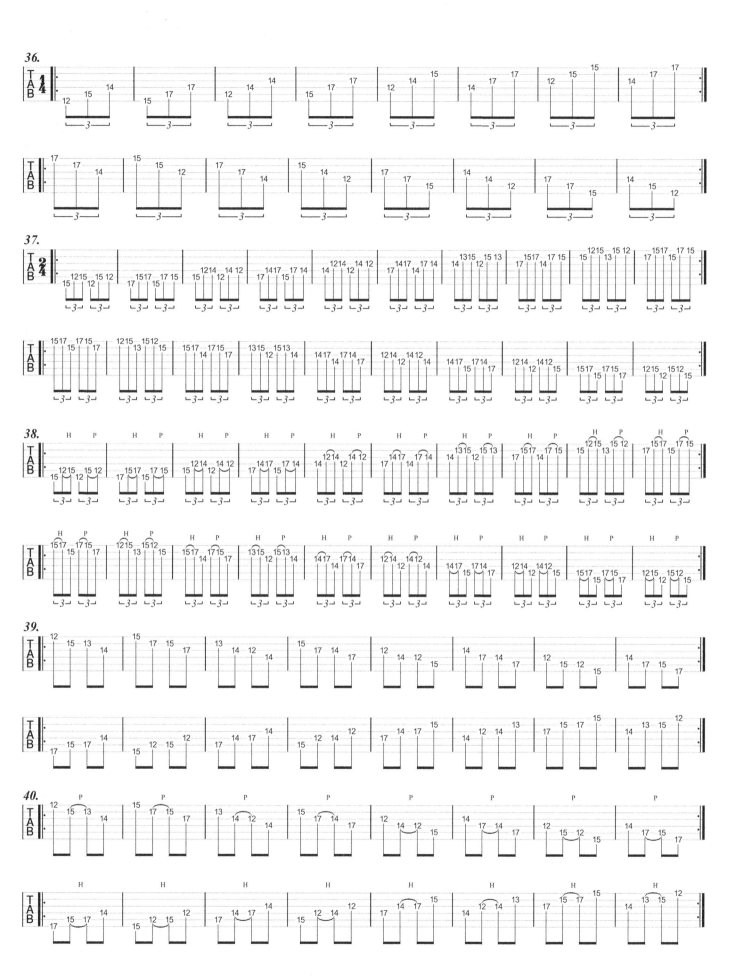

41.

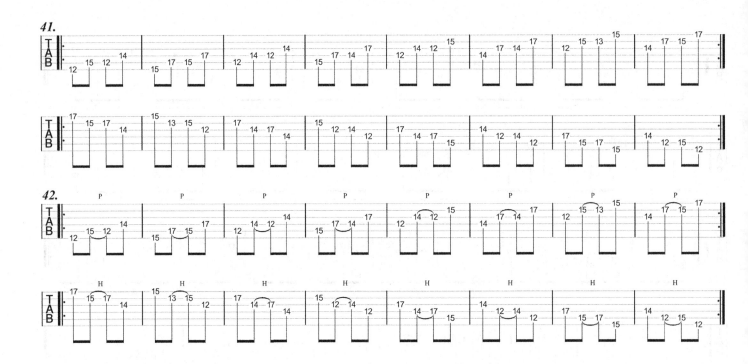

42.

Pentatonic Scales 5 & 1 Connected Patterns

Practice these two scales with alternate picking, then with hammer-ons and pull-offs, ascending and descending, before proceeding to the next section. Pentatonic scale 5 from the 3rd fret and pentatonic scale 1 from the 5th fret.

Pentatonic scale 5

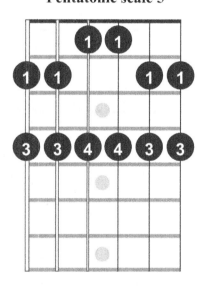

Pentatonic scale 1

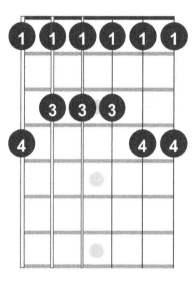

In the last section, we left off on scale 5, which brought us up to fret 17. This is getting pretty high up on the fretboard for some guitarists, depending on the type of guitar you are using. So, the exercises below have been brought down an octave, and they are still in the key of Am or C major. Keep in mind that you can relocate a scale an octave higher or lower when playing the exercises in other keys.

In each example, pentatonic 5 starts with frets 3-5 and pentatonic 1 starts with 5-8.

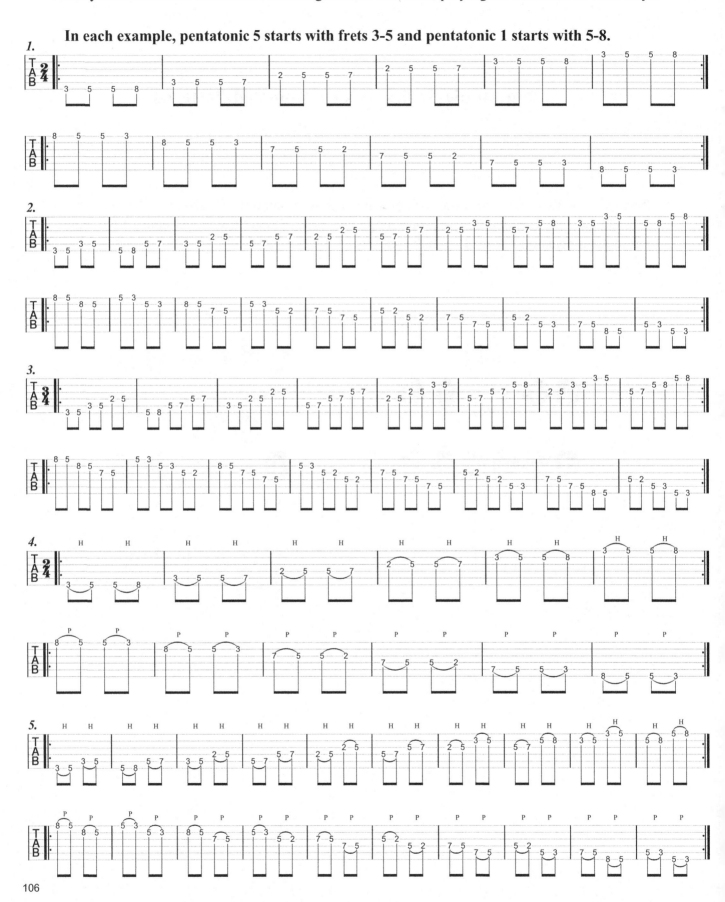

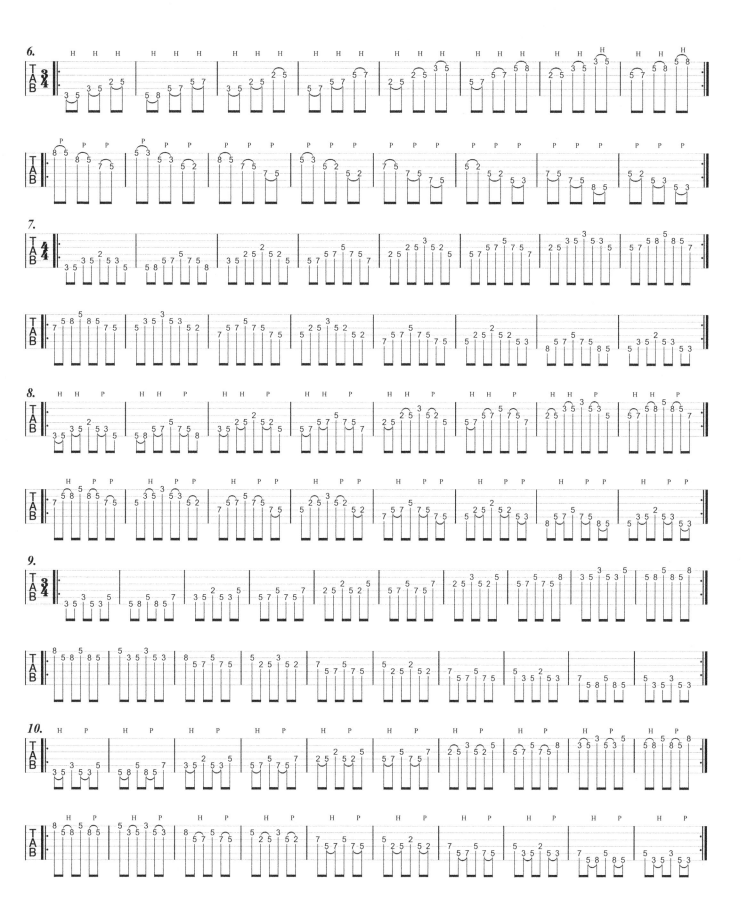

107

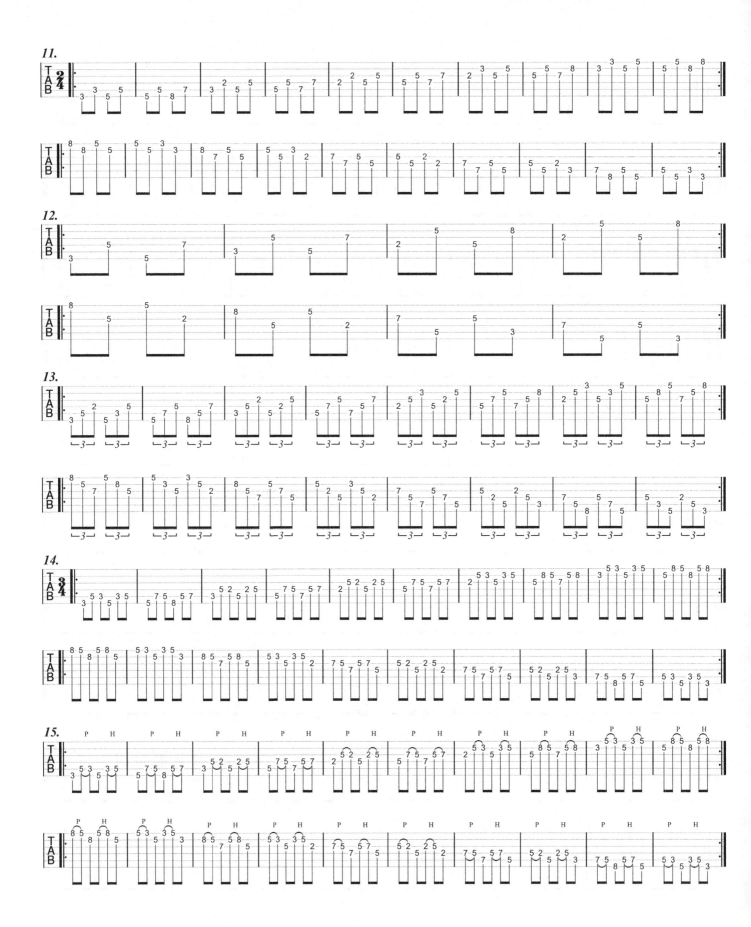

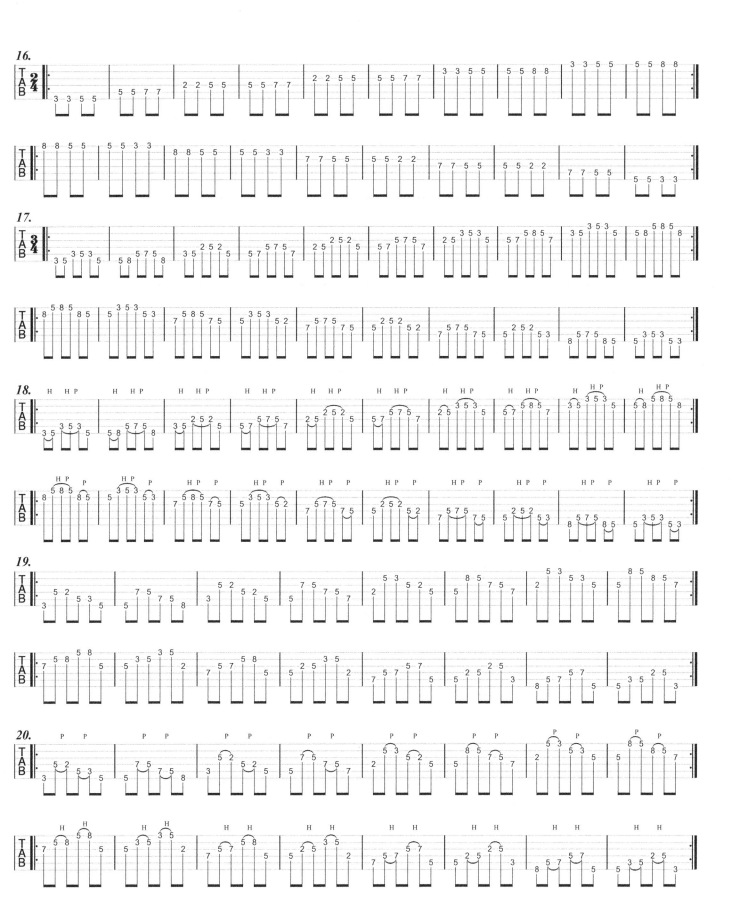

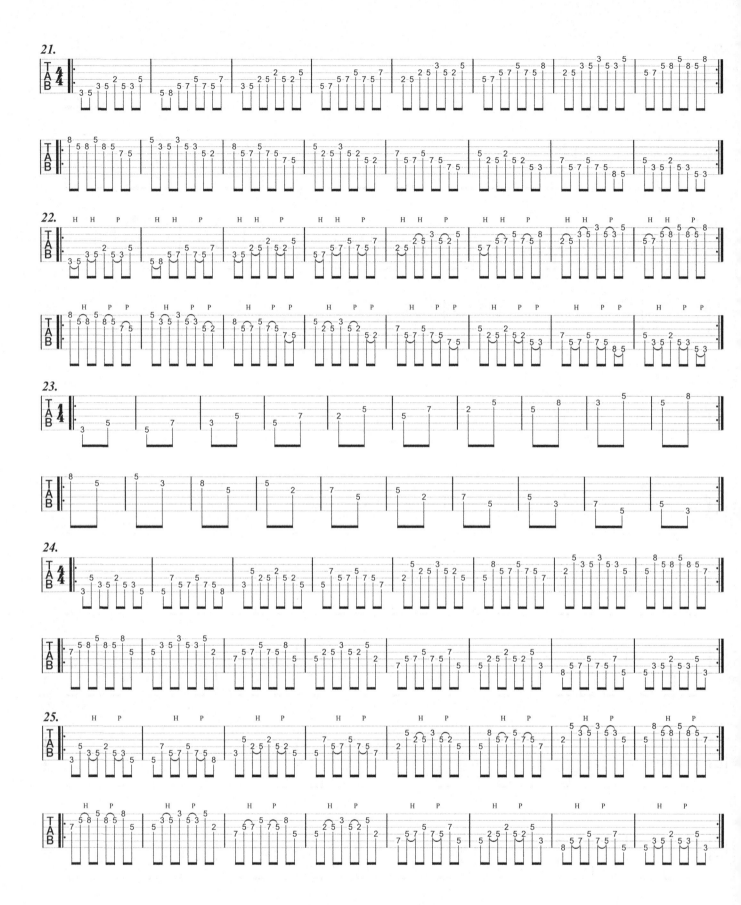

110

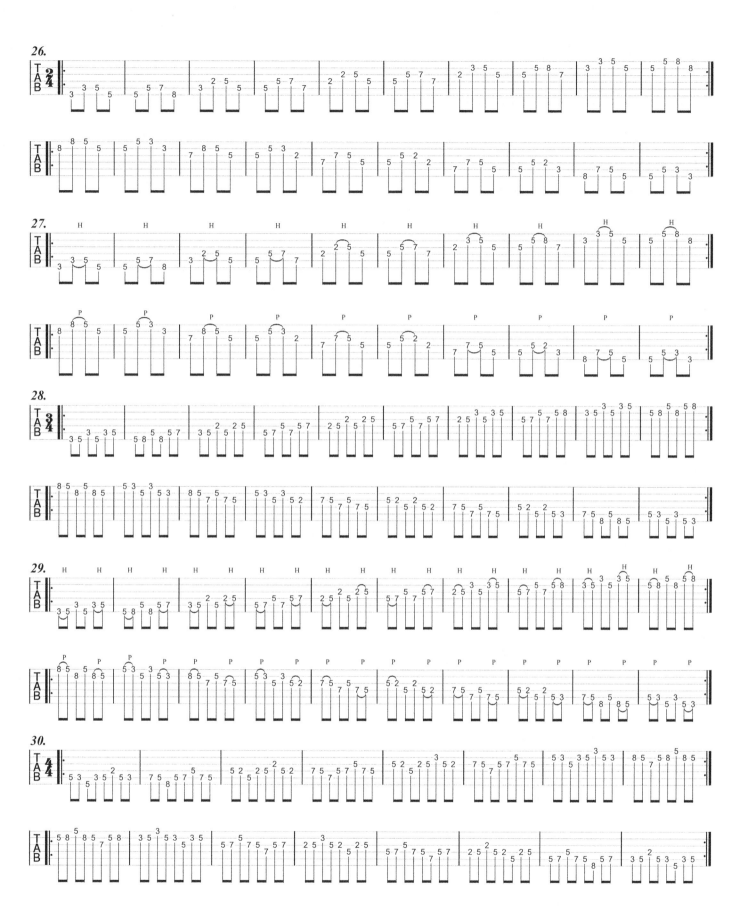

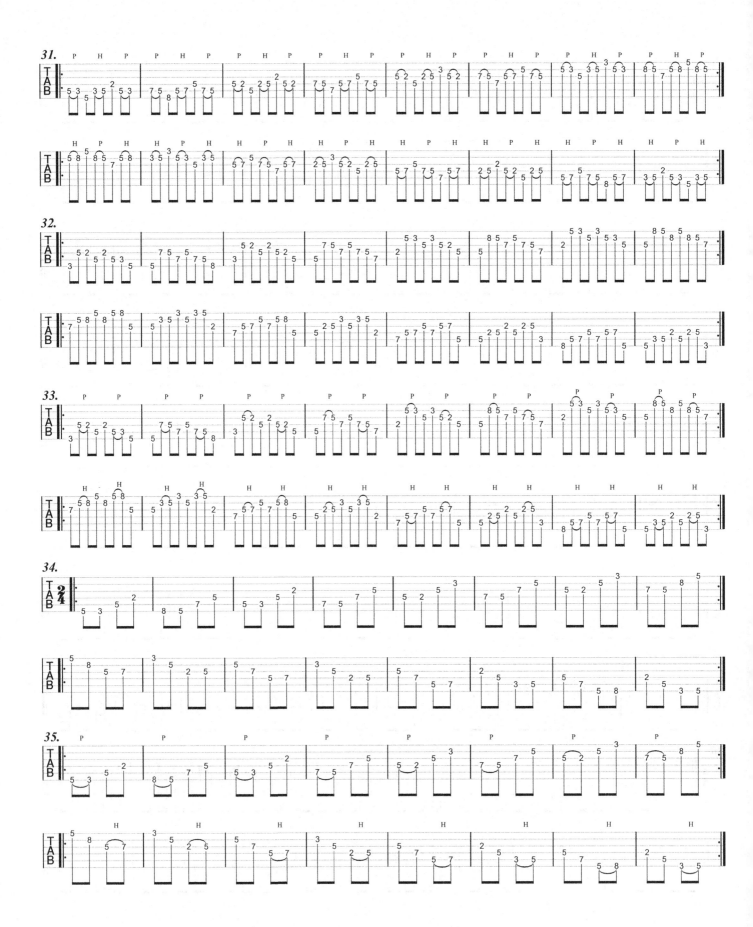

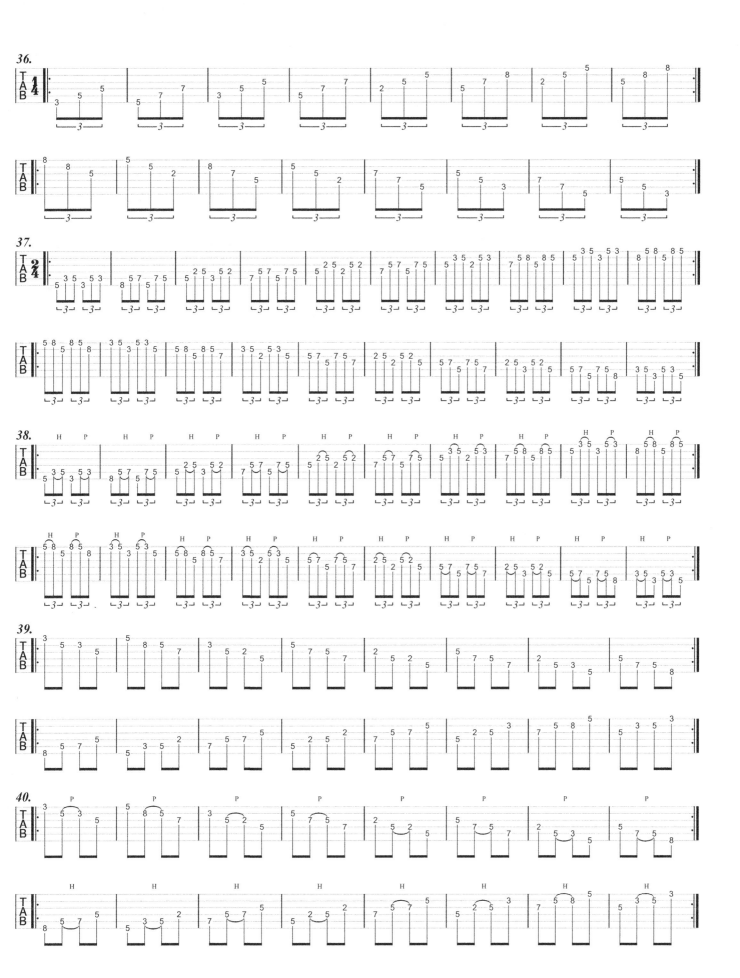

41.

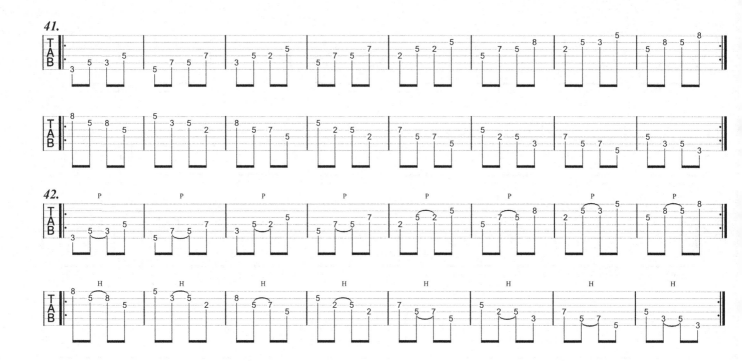

42.

Combined Pentatonic Scales - 3 Notes per String

As you play ascending through these scales, you will hear the notes under the 4th finger and 1st finger on the next string over are the same. This has a unique effect when you play quickly through the patterns. These 3 note per string patterns are also very good fret-hand exercises. If you have any experience with other 3 note per string scales like modes, then these patterns will complement them perfectly..

Practice with alternate picking, economy picking, hammer-ons, and pull-offs. Try them first around the 10th or 12th fret, because these patterns have a stretch to them!

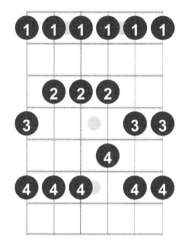

Pentatonic 1+2 or 5+1

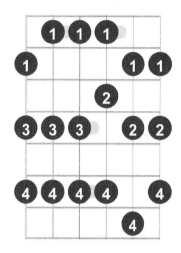

Pentatonic 2+3 or 1+2

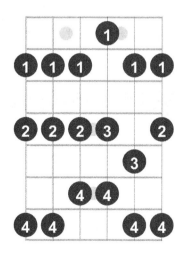

Pentatonic 3+4 or 2+3

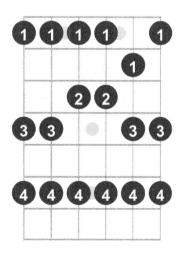

Pentatonic 4+5 or 3+4

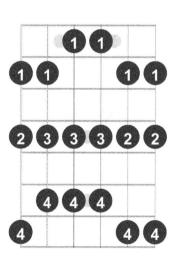

Pentatonic 5+1 or 4+5

Tip: These also make great tapping patterns! Try tapping wherever you see the 4th finger.

Open Pentatonic Scales

Open pentatonic scales are called open simply because they contain one or more open strings. These are the same scales used throughout this book, but they can be a little tricky to get used to. Practice them before going on to the exercises.

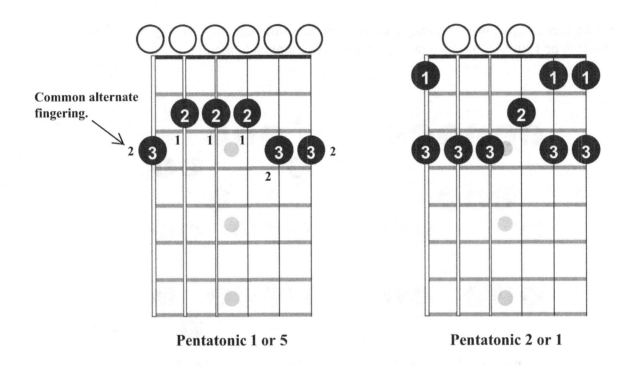

Pentatonic 1 or 5   **Pentatonic 2 or 1**

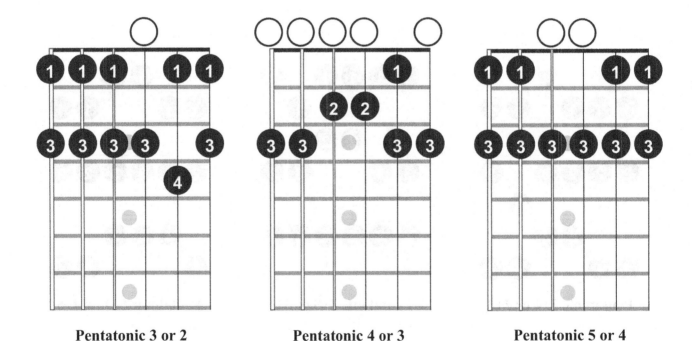

Pentatonic 3 or 2   **Pentatonic 4 or 3**   **Pentatonic 5 or 4**

Open Pentatonic Scale 1 or 5

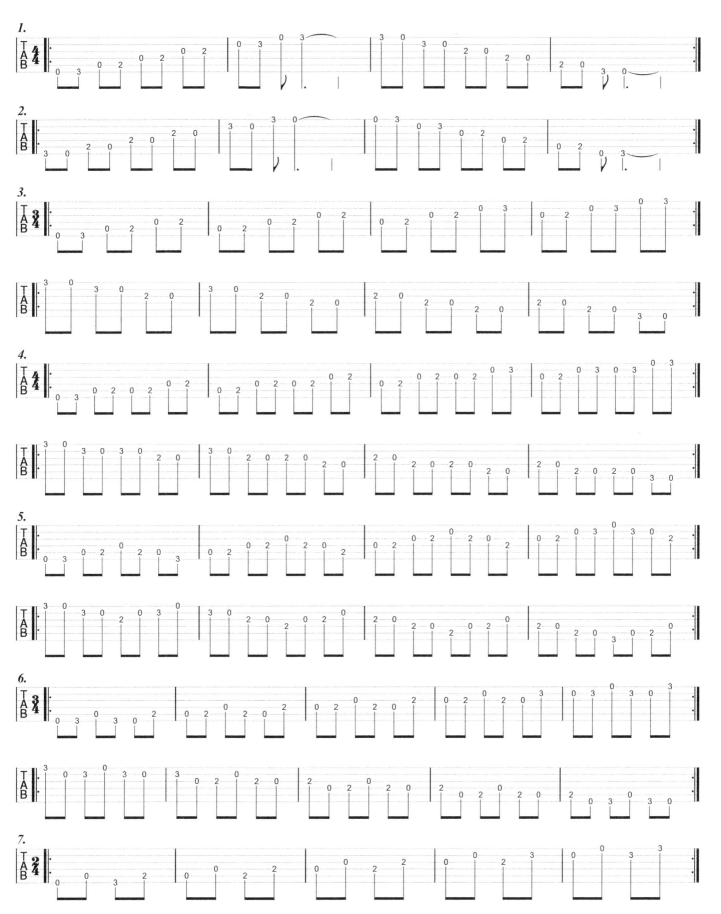

Continue next page.

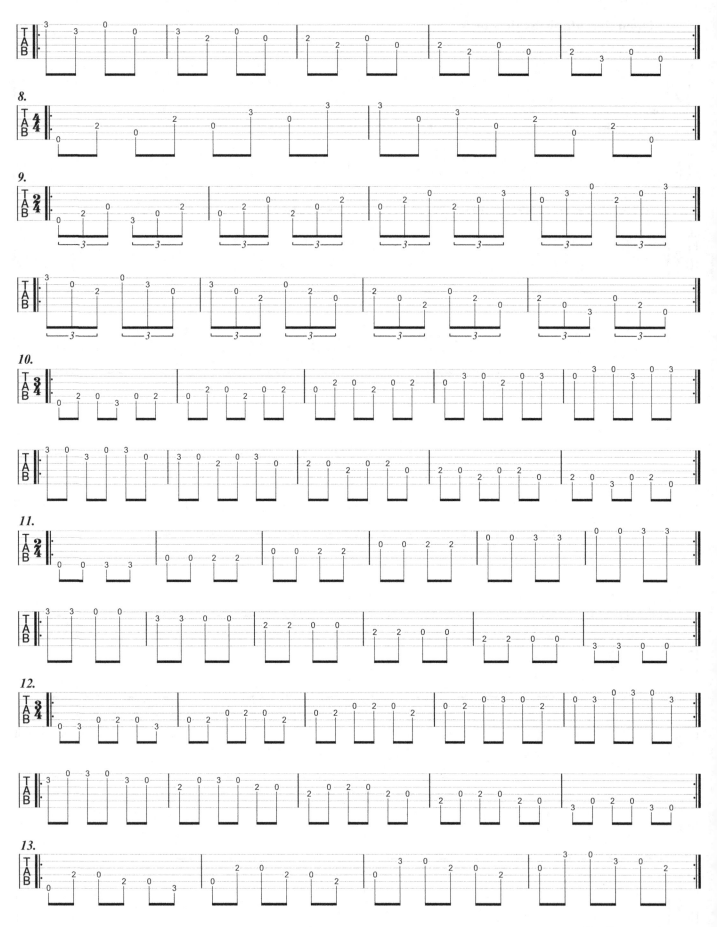

Continue next page.

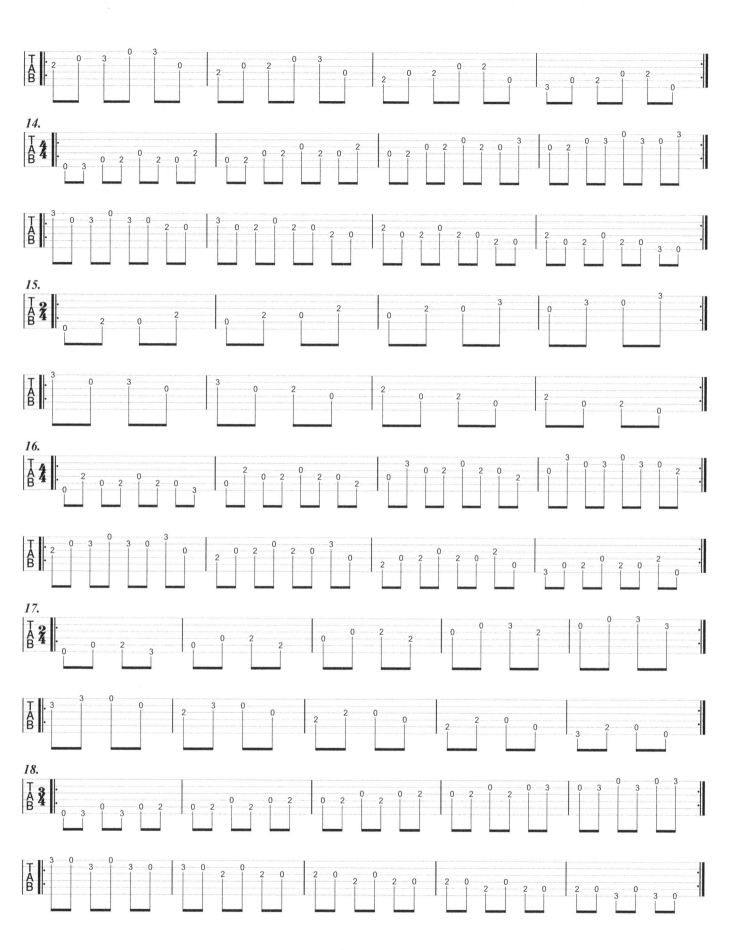

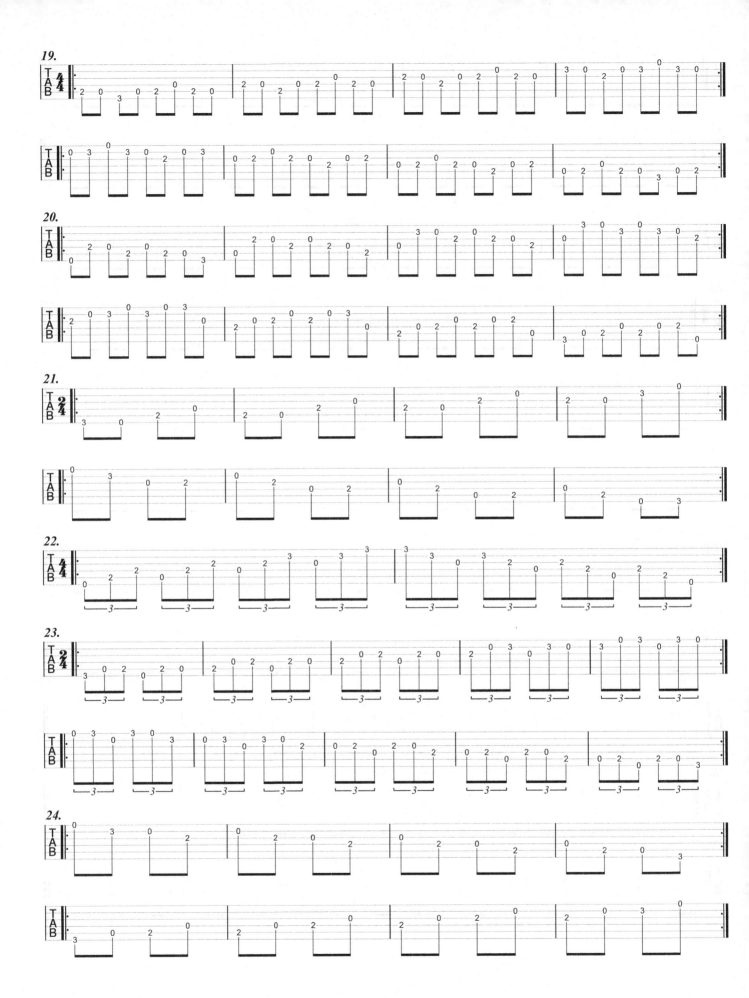

120

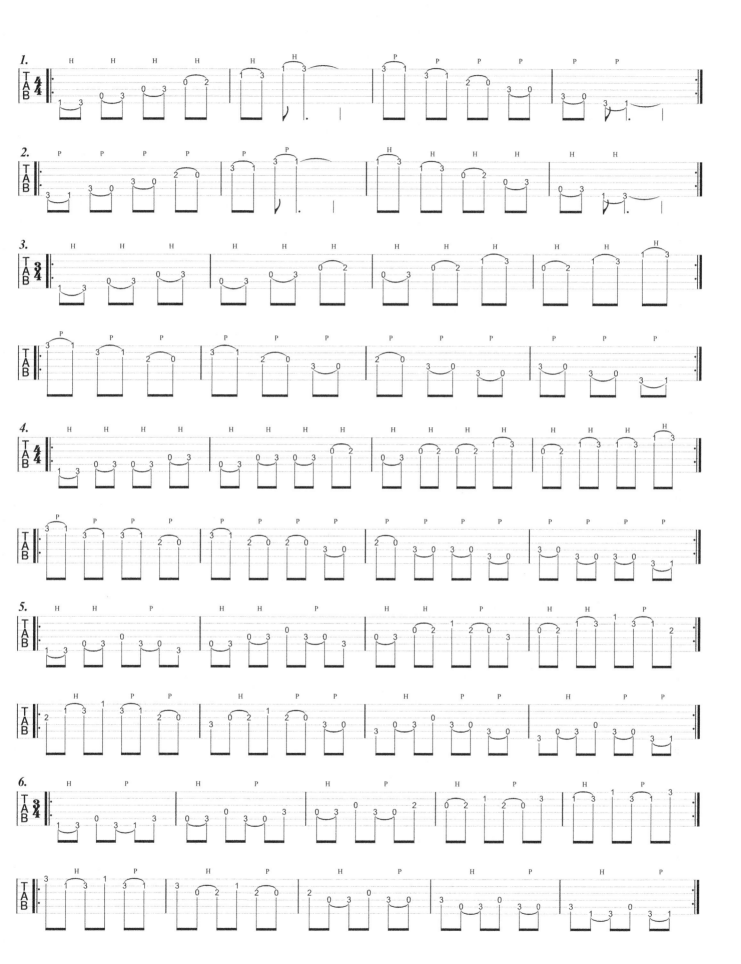

121

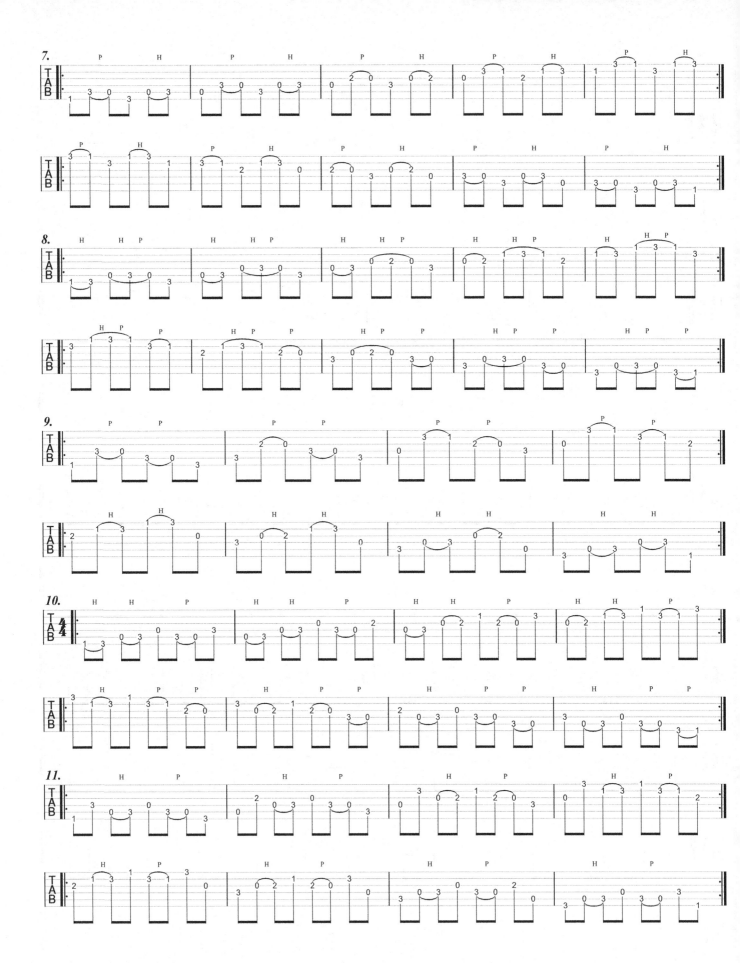

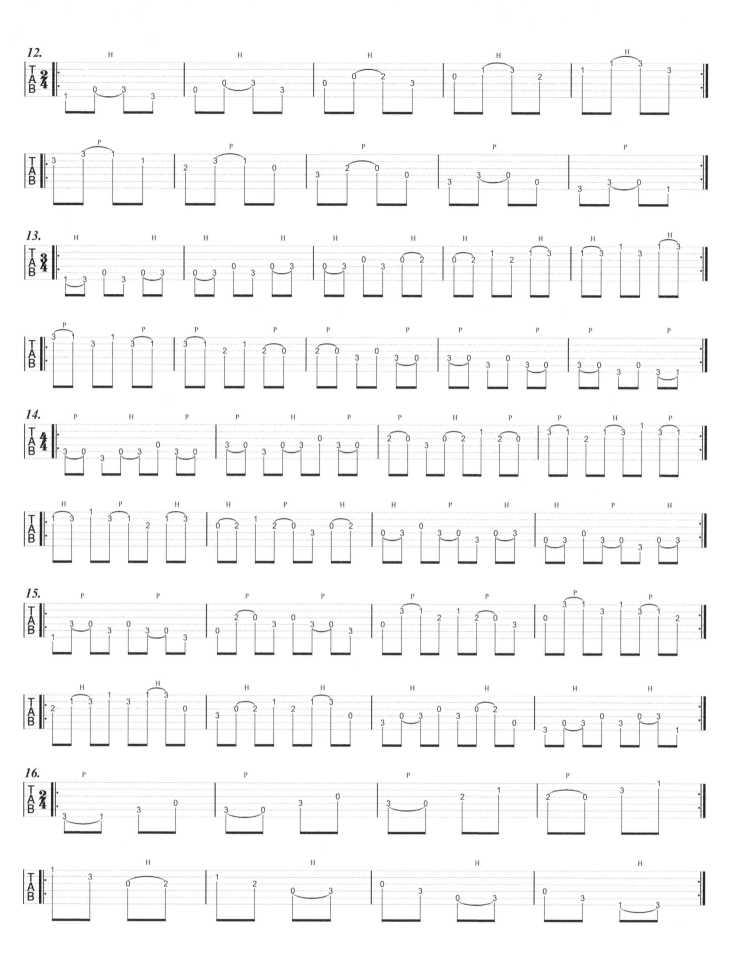

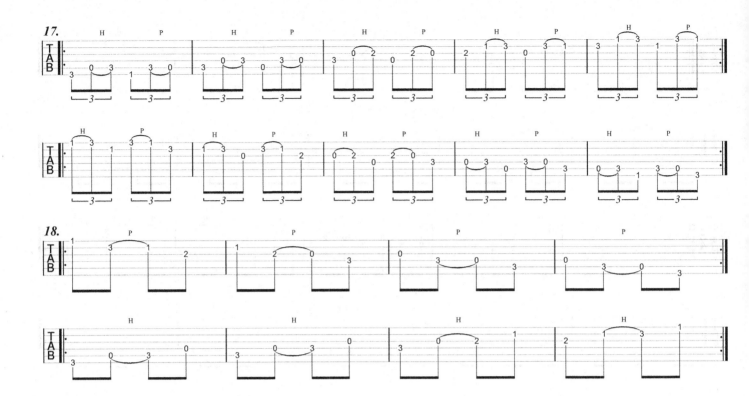

Open Pentatonic Scale 2 or 1

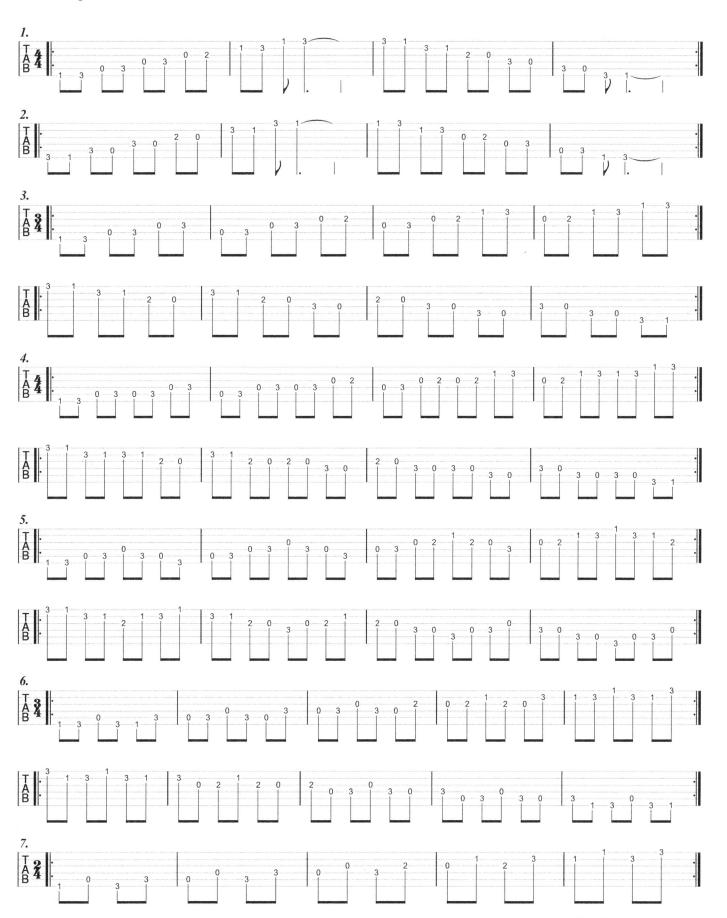

Continue next page.

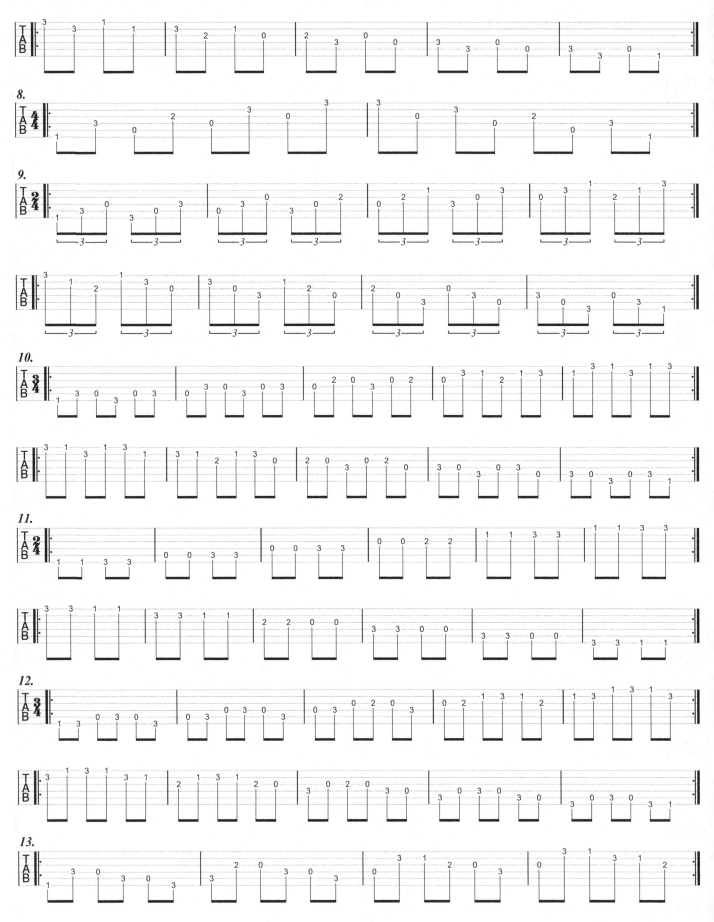

Continue next page.

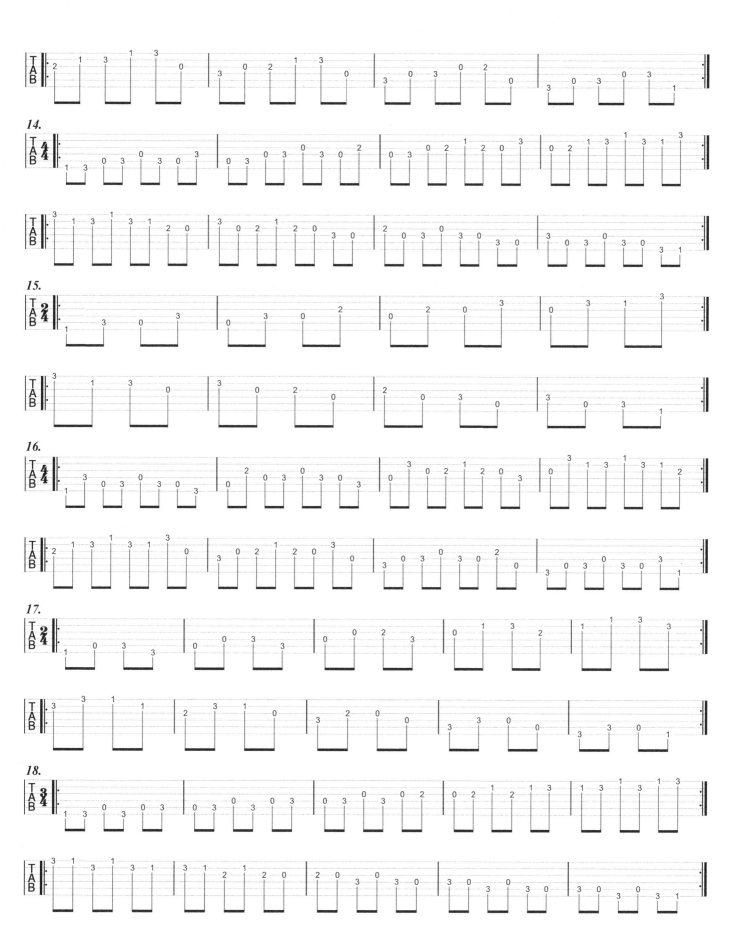

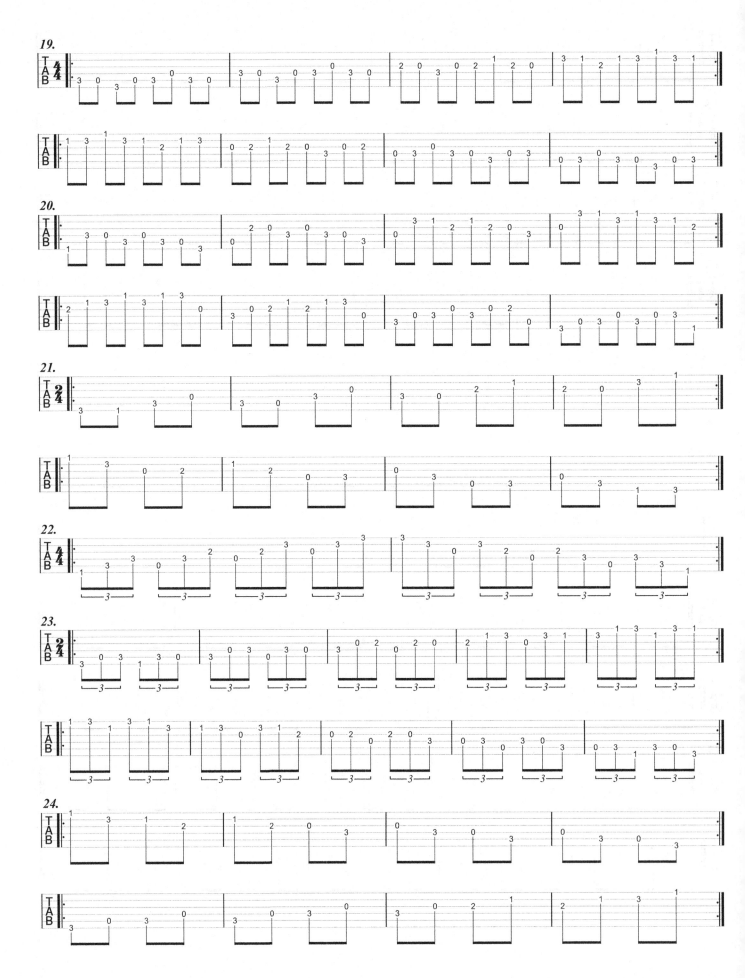

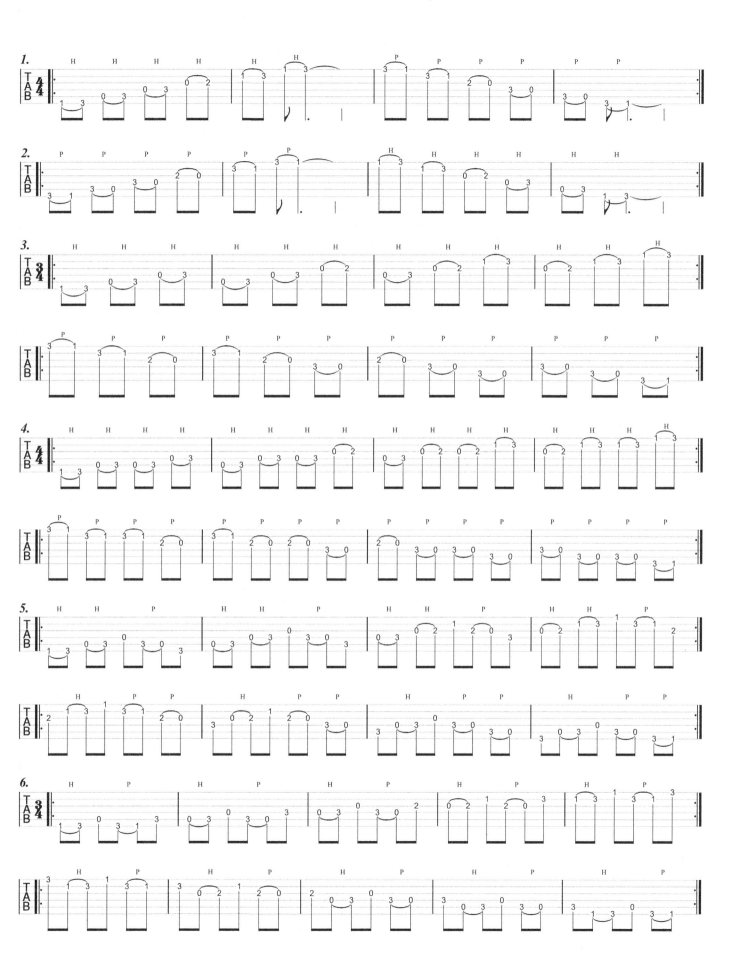

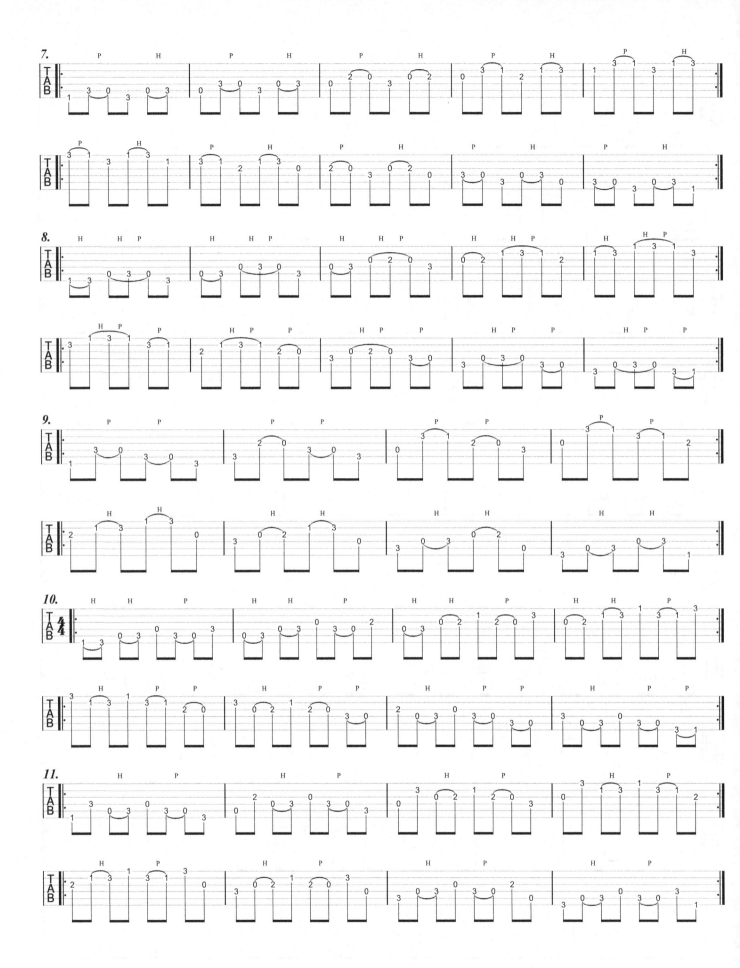

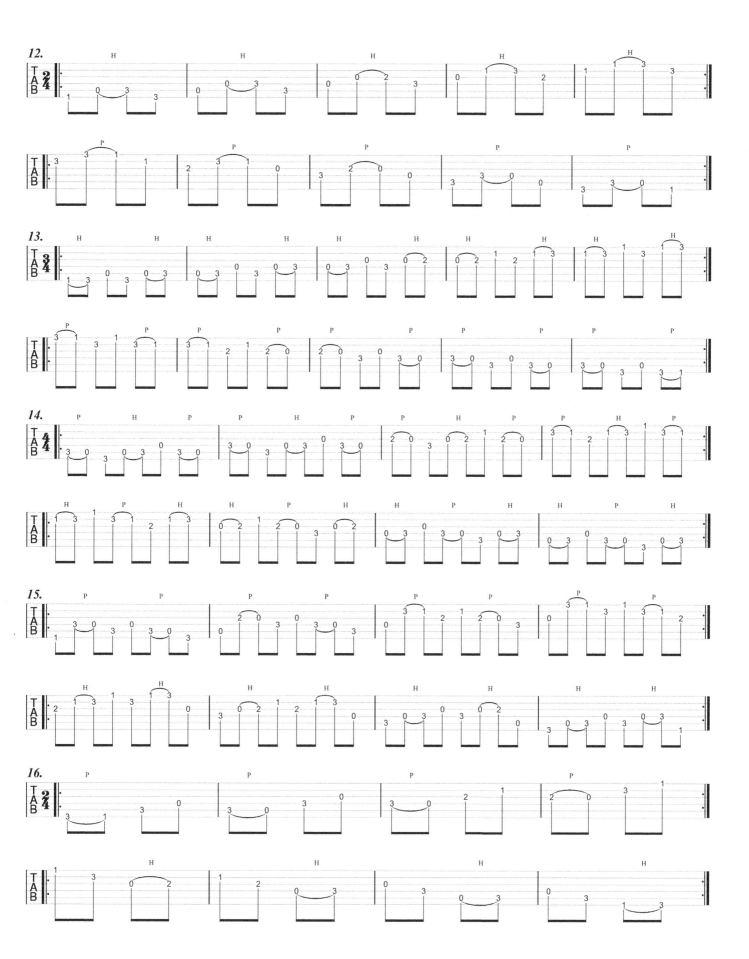

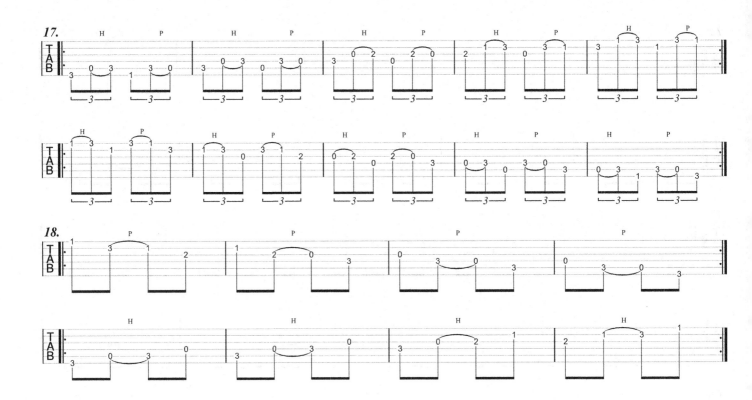

Open Pentatonic Scale 3 or 2

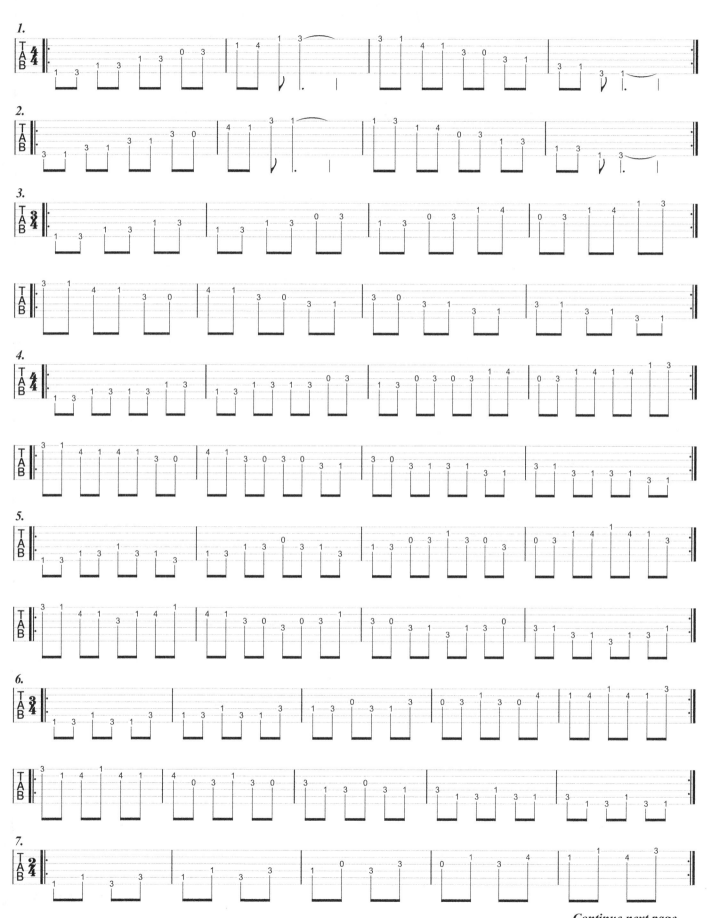

Continue next page.

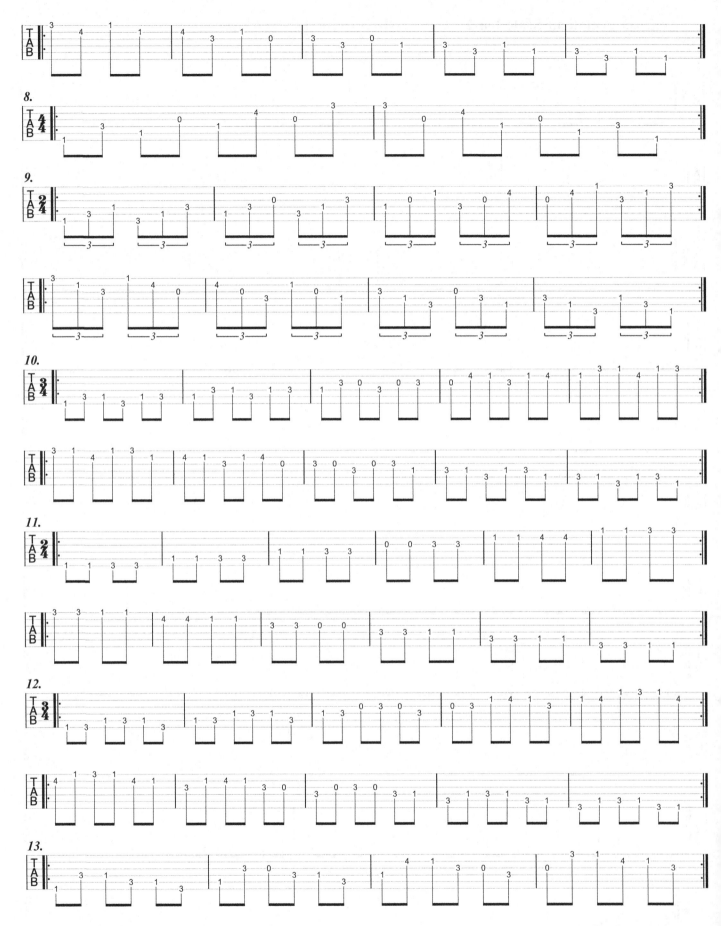

Continue next page.

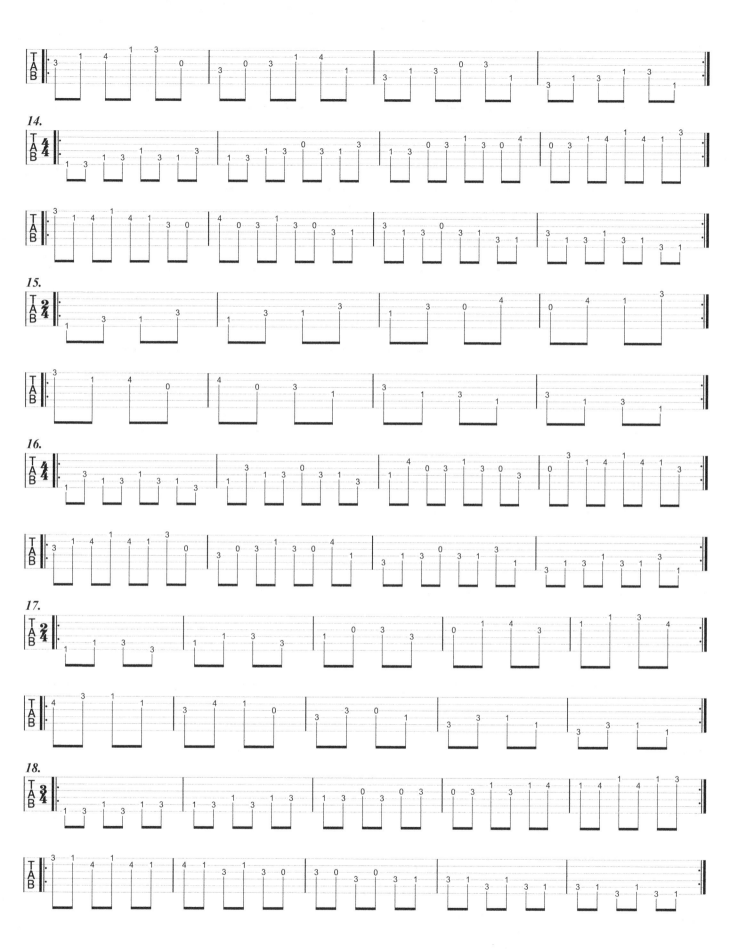

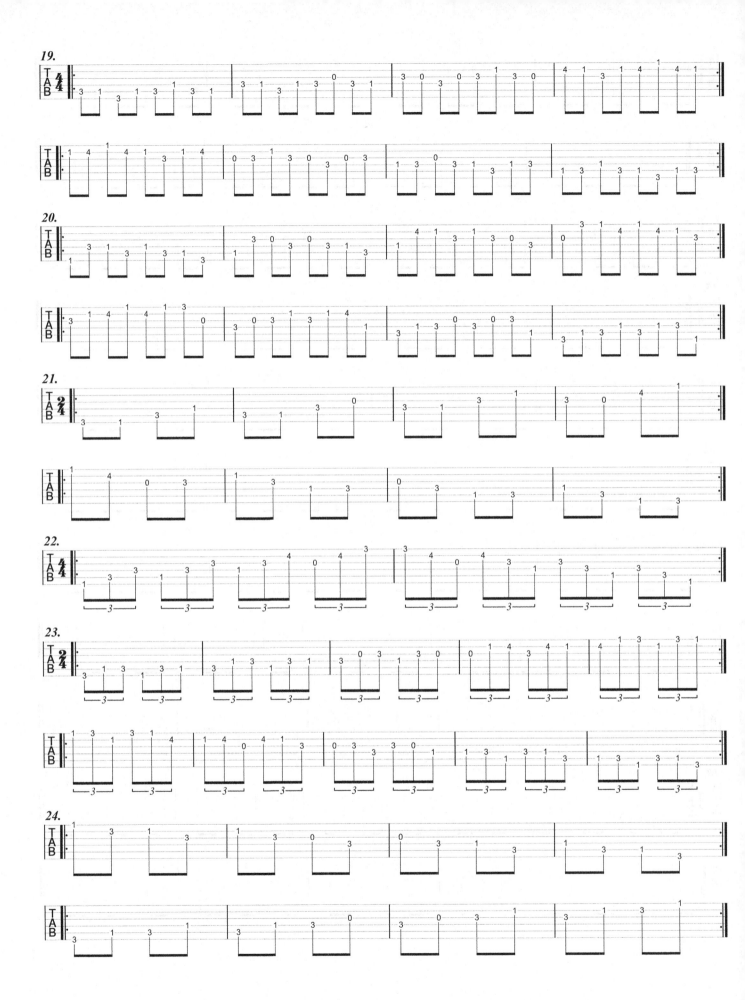

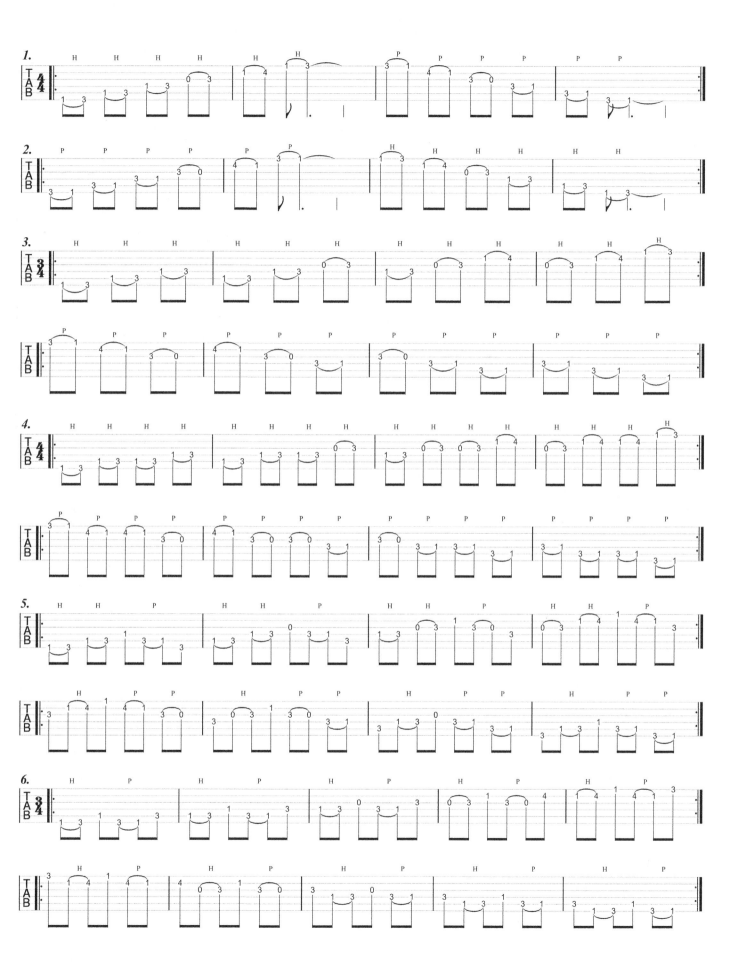

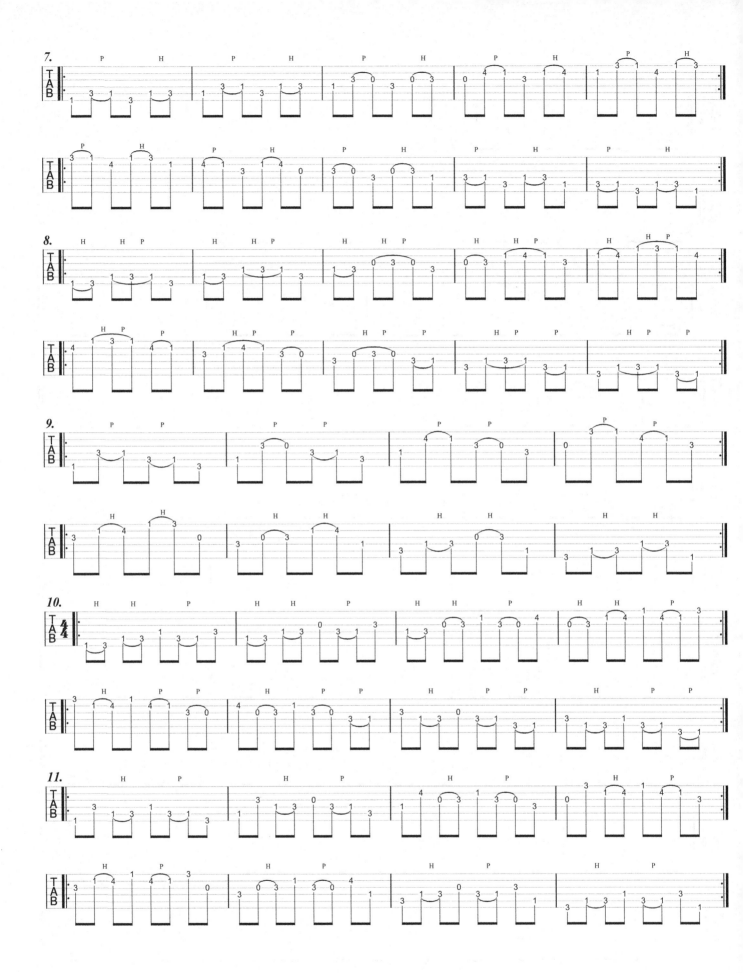

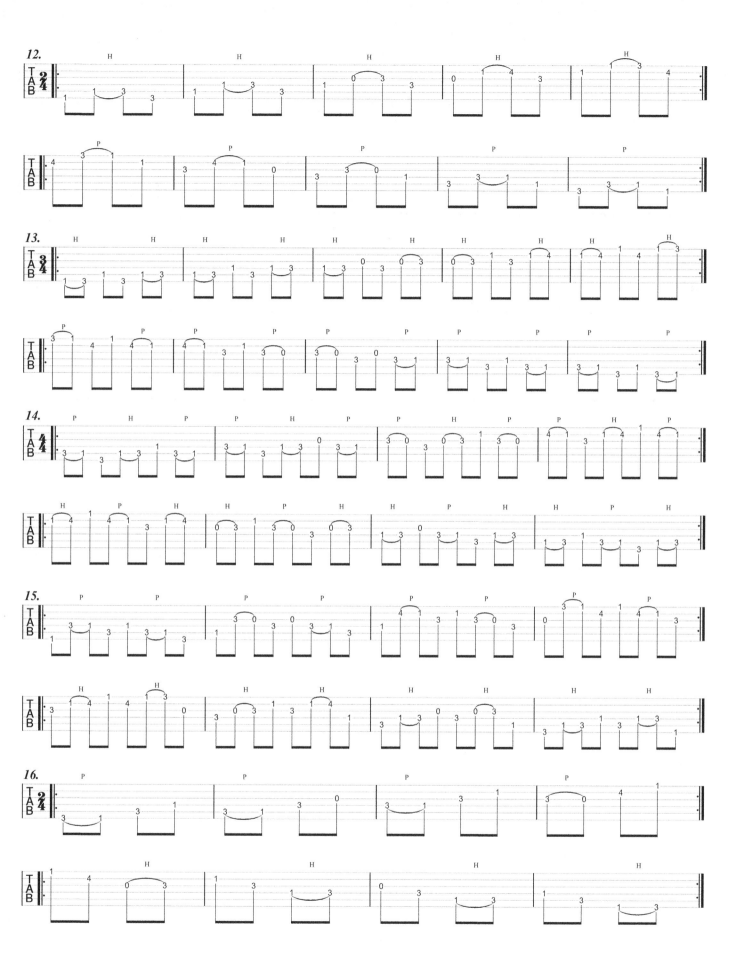

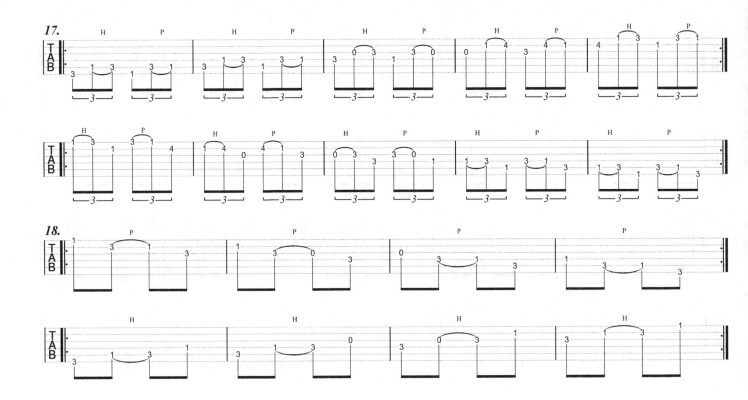

140

Open Pentatonic Scale 4 or 3

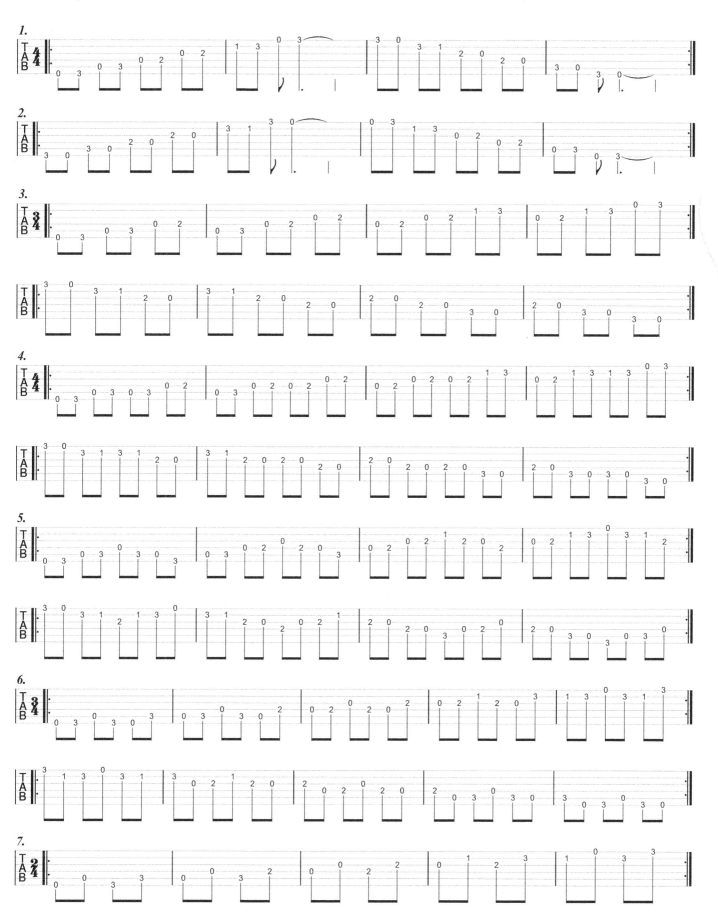

Continue next page.

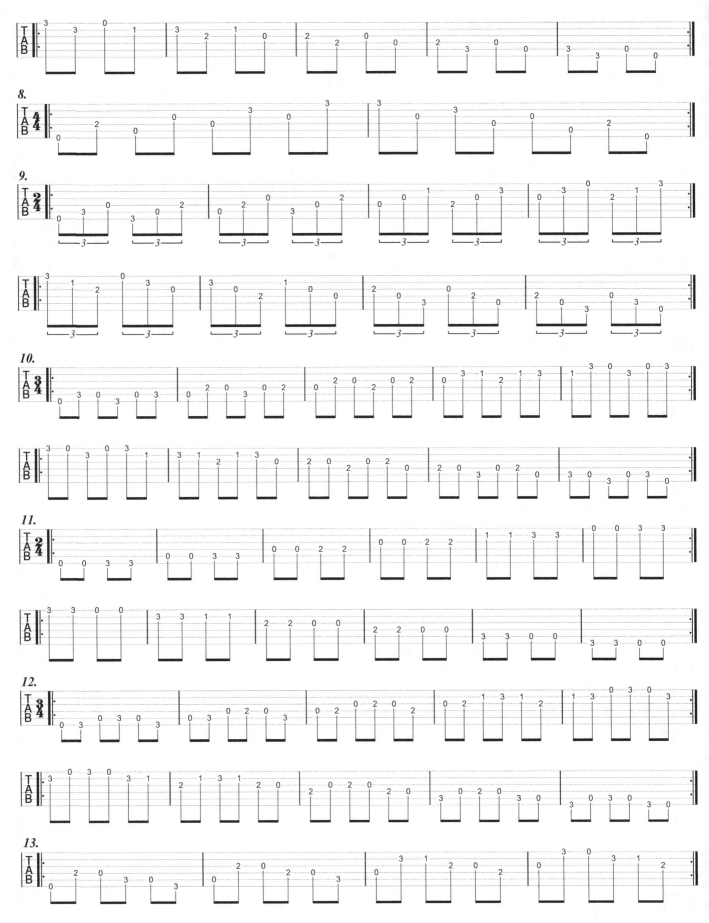

Continue next page.

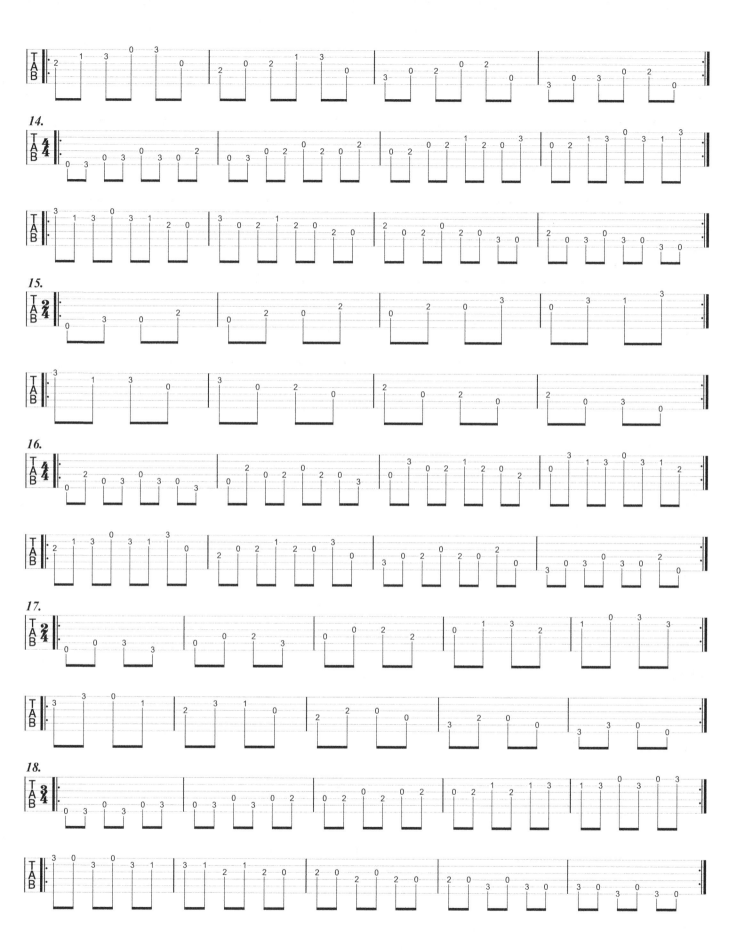

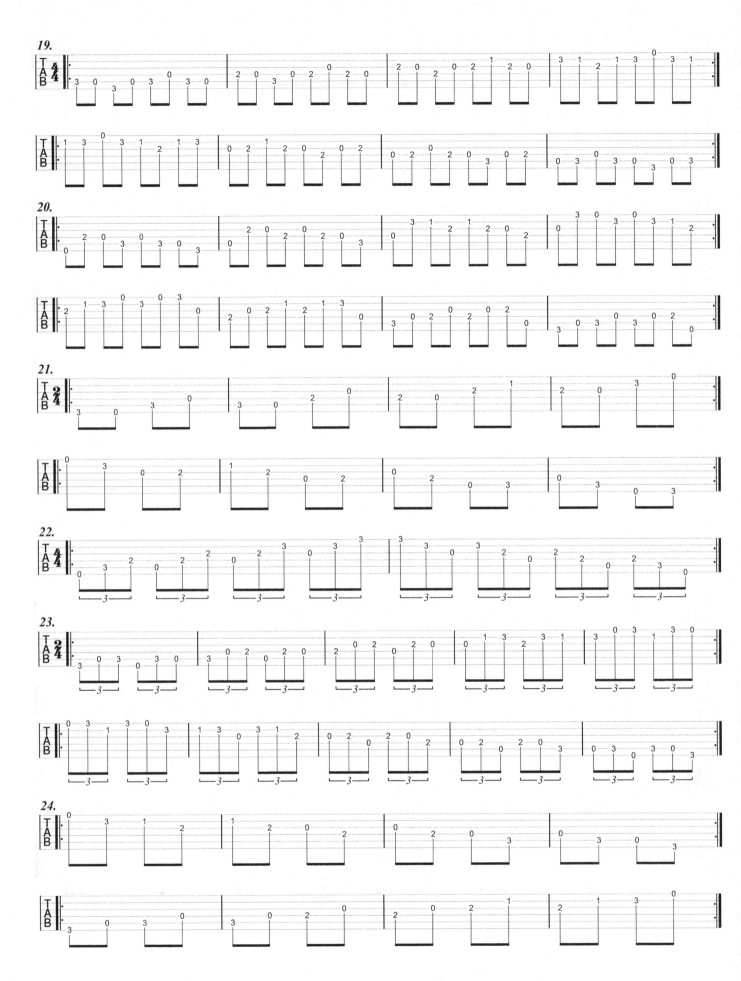

144

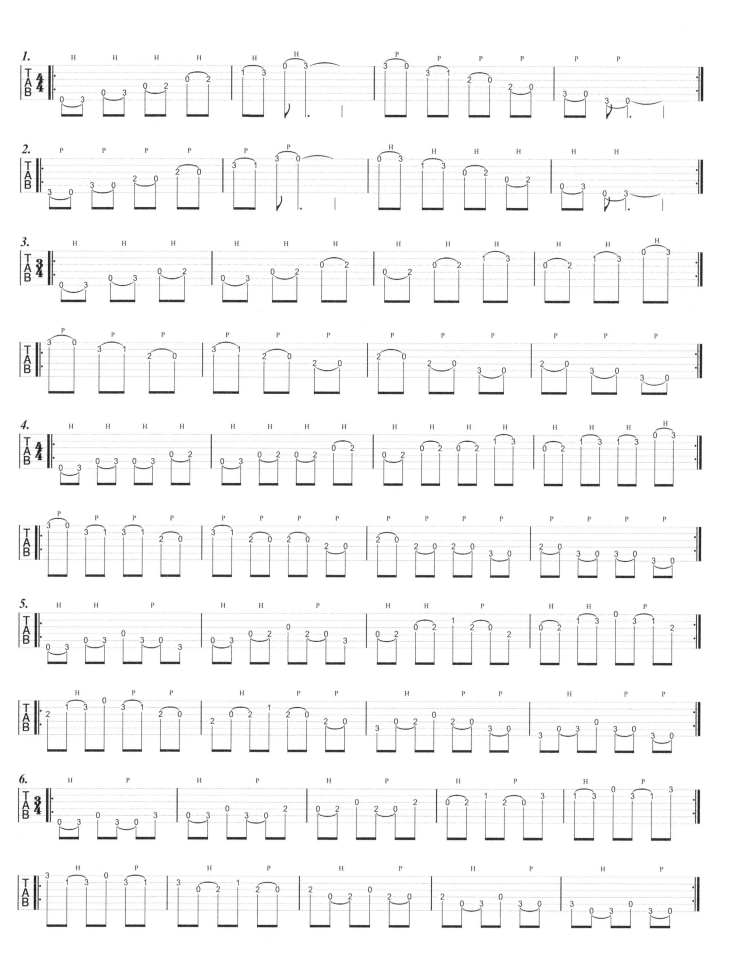

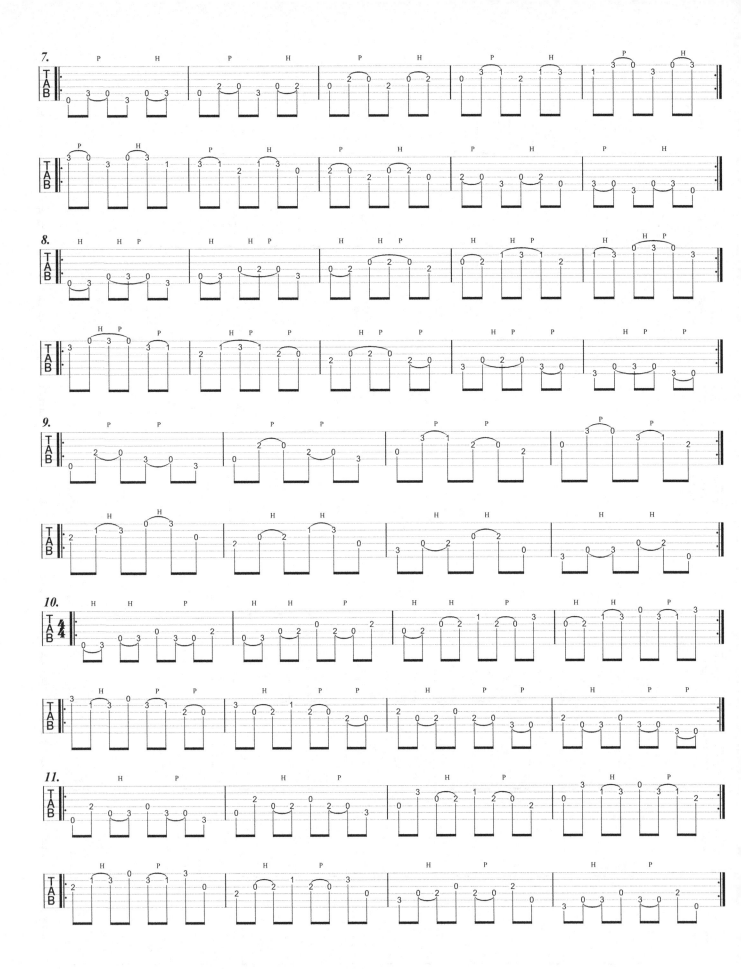

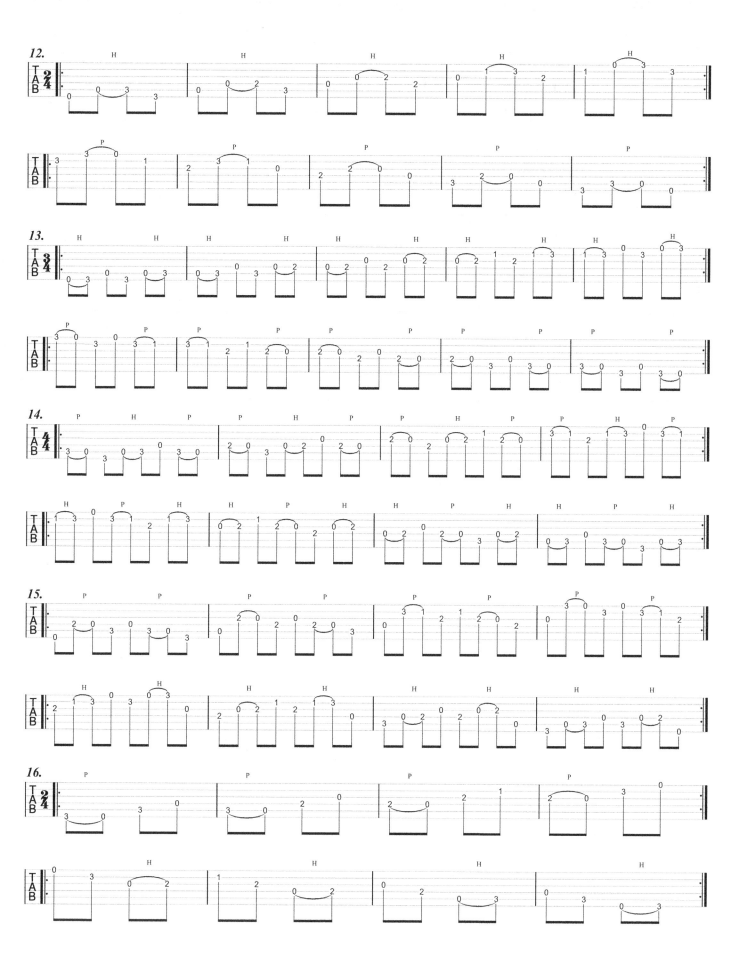

17.

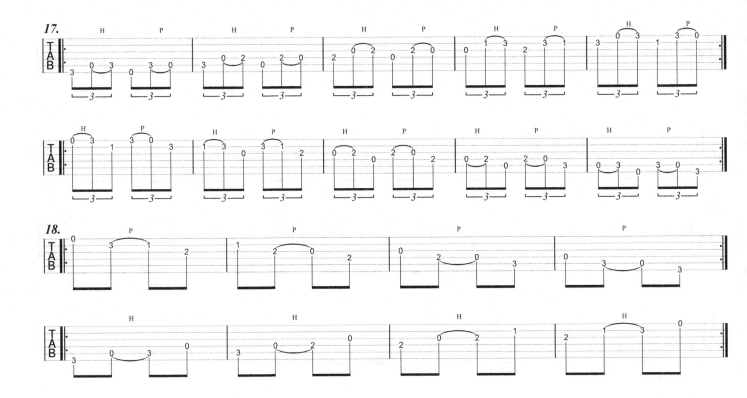

18.

Open Pentatonic Scale 5 or 4

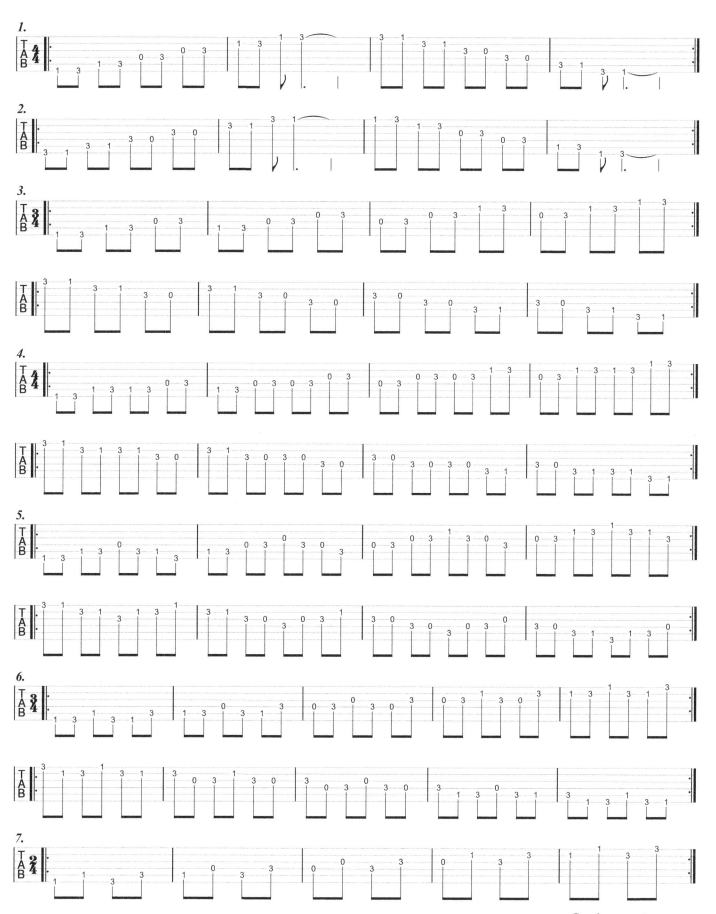

Continue next page.

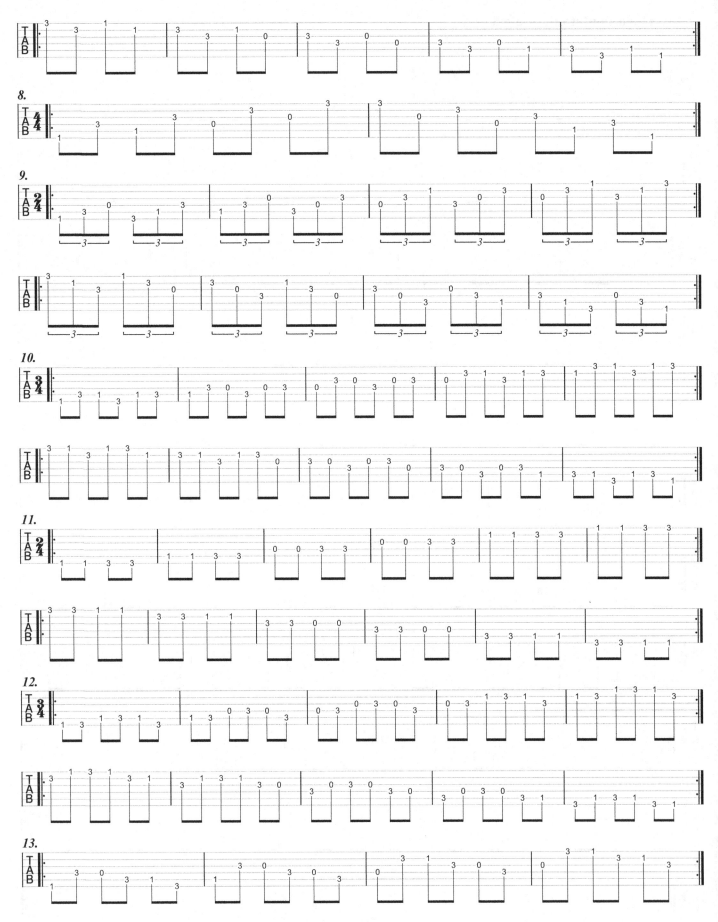

Continue next page.

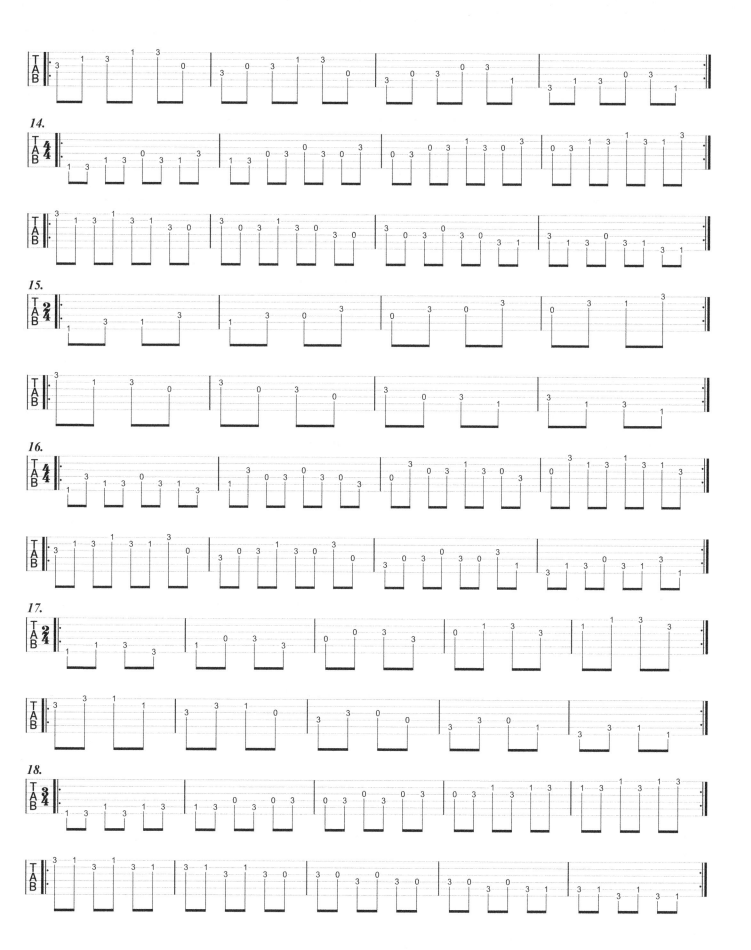

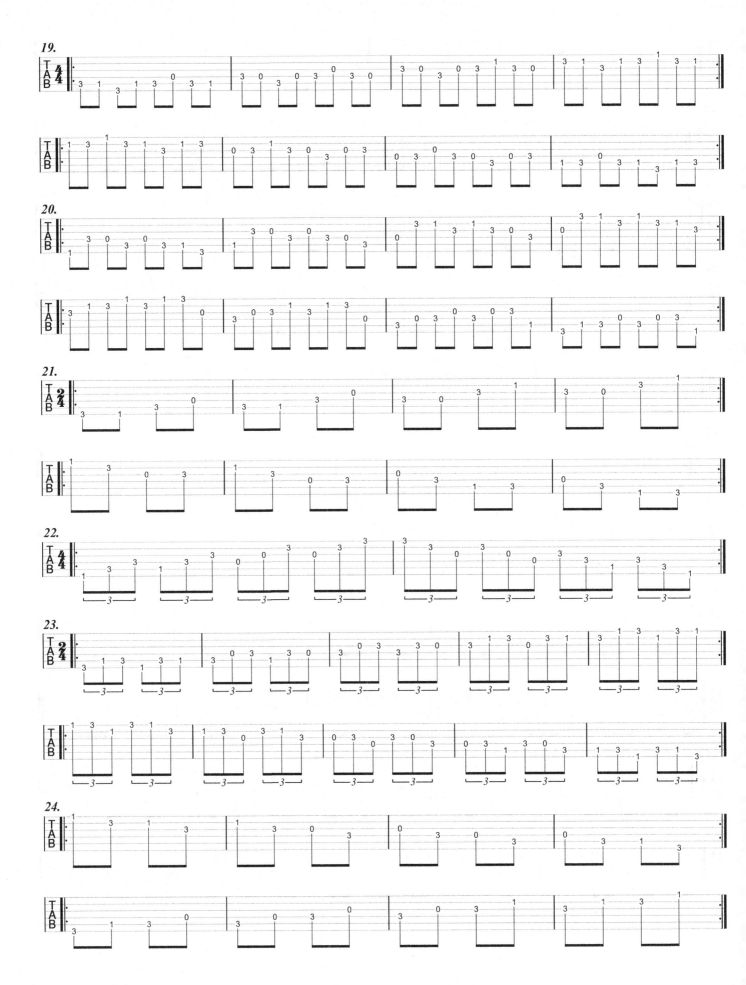

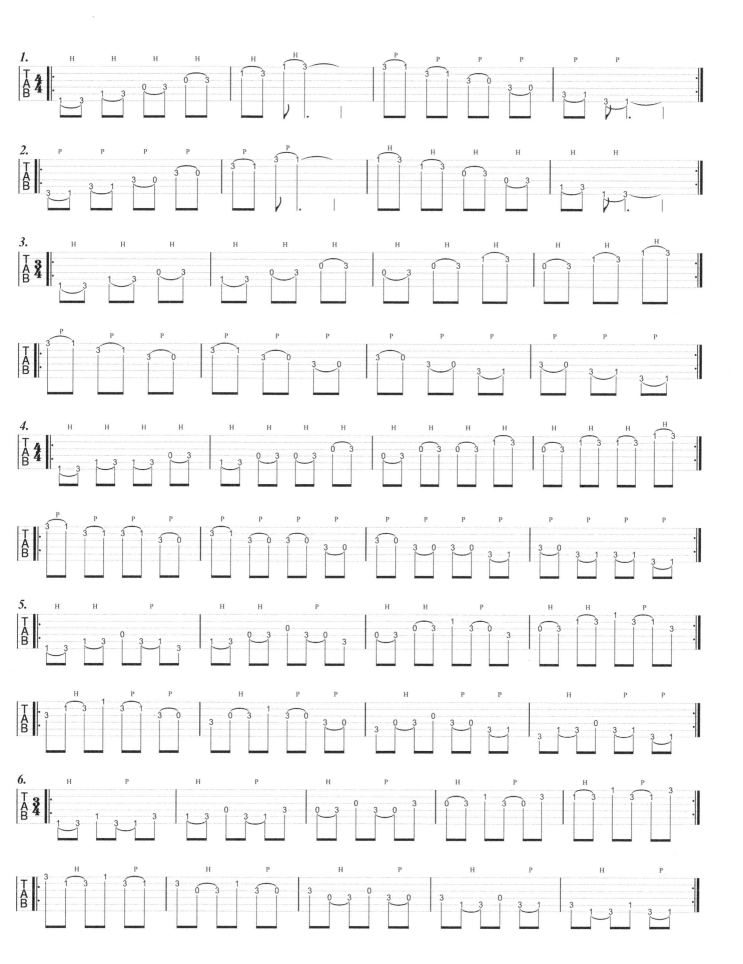

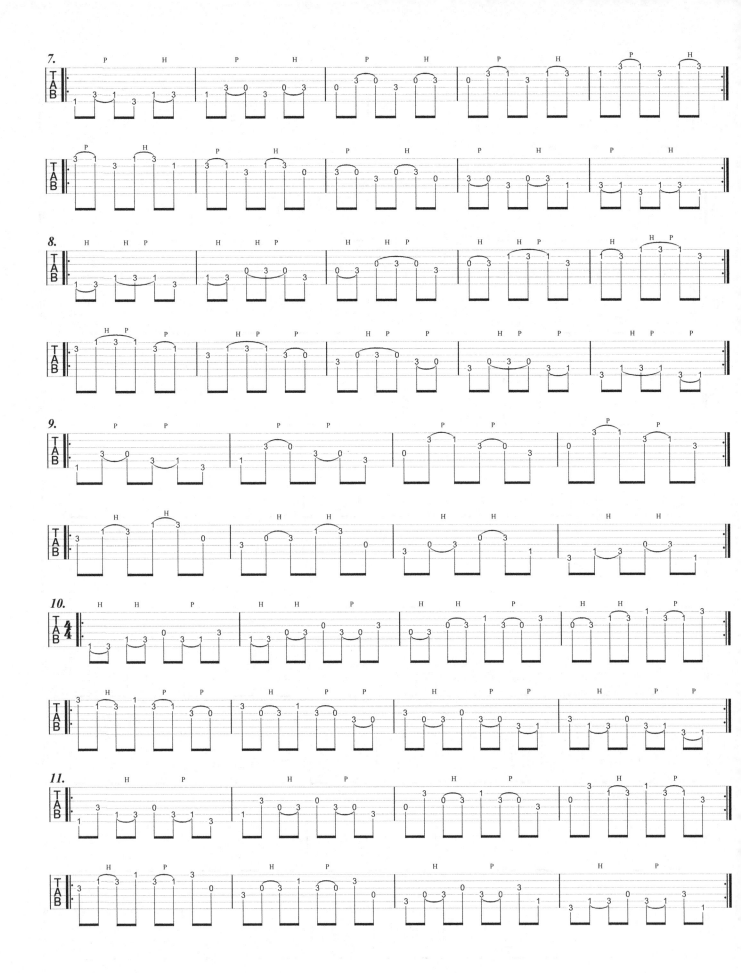

154

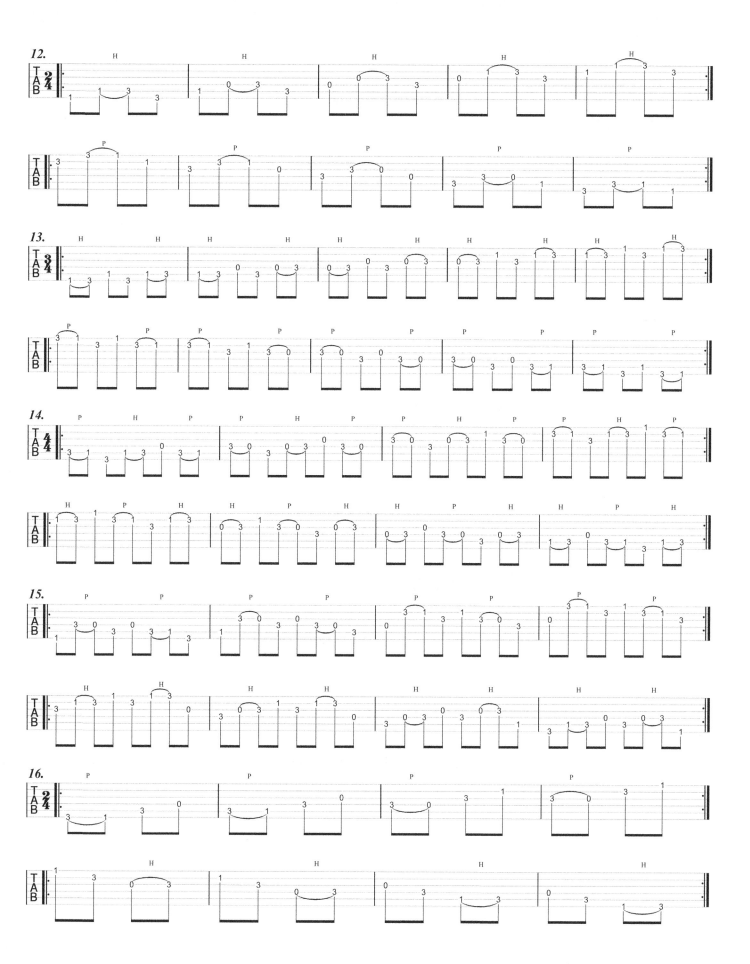

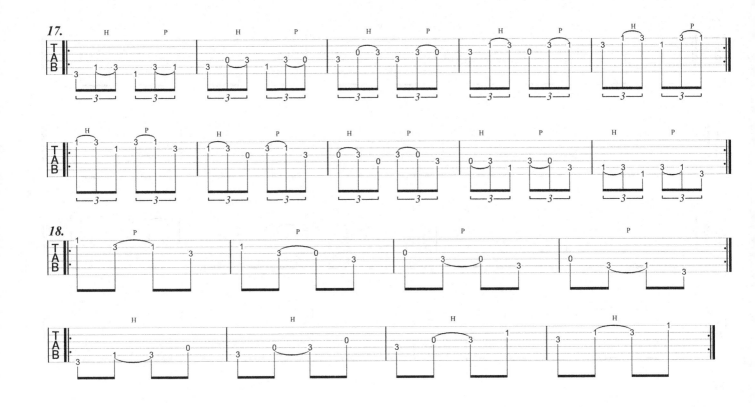

Thank you for your support!

For more information and a perfect companion to this book, visit:

All About Blues Guitar at

www.allaboutguitarbooks.com

Made in the USA
Monee, IL
25 September 2024

66547551R00090